CONTINUOUS ENERGY, & Upcoming Earth Changes

By Michael L. Schuster

First Edition
Sufra Publications, Milwaukee, Wisconsin

CONTINUOUS ENERGY,
& Upcoming Earth Changes
By Michael L. Schuster

Published by:

Sufra Publications
Post Office Box 16290
Milwaukee, WI 53216-0290

Library of Congress Catalog Card Number: 90-71287

ISBN 0-9627390-3-0: $14.95 Softcover

Printed in the United States of America
First Edition

Acknowledgments

My sincere thanks to "Clark", my favorite spook; the late Jane Roberts for bringing us the Seth material; Robert Butts for his many dedicated hours of transcribing that material; Kathleen Schoenstadt for her friendship & introduction to "Clark"; Mark Giese for his continual support; Serge Grandbois for his far reaching channeling; "Anderson" for the multidimensional networking; Robert Dubiel for his friendship and insightful regressions; Gerry Bowman for his powerful initiation in the great pyramid; Beth Karish for the wondrous catalyst she is; Jeff McDowell for the 4th dimensional logo on the cover; Ed Ebert and John Klug for their technical support; and Karn Korek for her typing and organizational skills.

I am truly grateful to all of the above for their varied talents and how they magically fit into the production of this manuscript.

Cover logo of spacecraft the property of Jeff McDowell.

Cover design and drawings of Einstein & Tesla created by Ben Denison.

About The Author

Michael Schuster has traveled throughout the U.S. and Canada discussing his death experience and the awesome soul perspective he encountered. He is a recognized spokesperson for a multitude of channeled material, as well as his vivid reincarnational insights and out-of-body experiences.

He is an available spokesperson for many facets of the new age and is open to setting up a talk or workshop in your area. Topics covered in workshops include an exploration of earth changes, personal issues of recognizing emotional blocks, opening up to a soul perspective and clarification of life focus. Please write to Sufra Publications for further information.

As indicated throughout the manuscript, "Continuous Energy" is the first book of a series dealing with various perspectives of "Moving into the 4th Dimension".

Comments on the manuscript or your reaction to the exercises are especially welcome.

TABLE OF CONTENTS

– TABLE OF CONTENTS –

CHAPTER FOUR – "RENEWABLE ENERGY"

CHAPTER FIVE – "DIRECTED THOUGHT"

CHAPTER SIX – "CIRCUITS OF INTENT"

CHAPTER SEVEN – "THE NEUTRON"

CHAPTER TEN – "A UNIFIED FIELD OF THOUGHT"

CHAPTER ELEVEN – "A VIBRATIONAL SHIFT"

– TABLE OF CONTENTS –

CHAPTER FIFTEEN – "ET'S & THE PYRAMIDS"

CHAPTER SIXTEEN – "CELLULAR MEMORY"

CHAPTER EIGHTEEN – "FORMATTING YOUR INTENT"

CHAPTER NINETEEN – "WHAT CONSTITUTES REALITY?"

Introduction

(Under hypnosis)

"I'm still somewhat irritated by the whole journey. I'm piecing together what I got out of this conference. Why did I come? There were many moments I enjoyed and I'm reflecting on all that. It's simply a matter of what I want to focus on, the irritation or the fun. I'm still irritated though. I'm getting on the airplane and I'm tired. It's the end of the trip. There's a woman in my seat! Now why is she in my seat? I'll ignore her and just sit down in the aisle seat. It's fine. She's got on a hat, a lot of dark clothing with vests and leather and wool. Her hat covers a good part of her face. The colorfulness of the materials shows between the leather. It's many layered.

Just looking at her begins to propel me out-of-body, not realizing it yet. I'm half in my body, half out of it. The plane is taking off, I'm clearly not there (on the plane). I'm worried about my body, how can I be in two places at once? There's some trauma here, but it's okay. I've bilocated many times before, why is this different? At this moment, the projection of the mother ship and the airplane are equal. I'm seeing the equality of the (space craft) experience and my physical focus. She's stabilizing my energy. Her eyes aren't physical. She's wearing physical clothing, she has a face. On the one hand, it was nondescript, and on the other, it wasn't even there! It's familiar energy and it's alien at the same time. I didn't realize while in my body that I knew her. While recognizing my dual focus, I am her! She's a reflection of who I am. It's a representation of my greater self, it's a middle ground between physical and nonphysical focus.

She began to propel me out-of-body the minute I got on that plane. I was veering from in body to out-of-body, but not consciously. There are no more than eight people on that plane, she would have been nine. But she wasn't there, nobody else saw her.

She was a projection, and from my altered state, I can see that nobody is in that seat. She's carrying on a dialogue with me out-of-body, explaining what's about to happen.

She is saying that she is a representation of who I am in physical focus. She is going to accompany me on a journey. We're floating above the airplane, carrying on this dialogue. Her greater sense of energy is not in that projection I saw on the airplane, but it's with me out-of-body. She's a swirling blue and white light, in many physical embodiments, and she's going back and forth. It's kind of amusing because I can make her anything I want by my own projection. I know that shes not from earth. I'm in an astral body, yet what's before me is way beyond astral. She's explaining that she's my teacher, but there's a very implicit understanding of our equality. We are one, but for terms of the projection, she is an individual. She's explaining that she will accompany me and we will actually hold hands.

I look back onto the airplane and I'm still reading the magazine, but that's not of interest to me now. I'm embraced in her energy. I'm within her energy as we take a journey through a time warp into another dimension. It's exciting and I'm remembering what I do in my dreams and altered states. There's nothing alien about it. It's fun. She's not physical, but the energy behind her projection has form. She "lets go" and we merge with the Orion energies. It's a different time and space, yet all connected in some way.

We are in a place that's "no place". It's futile to describe where I am. I understand that it's in a world of my mental body and my emotional body, but it's not a physical embodiment. It can be physical if I want it to be. I'm creating the space for the projection to "ride" in – along with the energy of the Orion presence and the "Sufra presence" . . . my greater self. I can focus on the space ship or I can focus on the light of her energy. I can go back and forth because I'm somewhat intimidated by the energy of the craft. It's immense! I don't know if I'm ready to behold the technology. The beings onboard represent many different facets of consciousness.

I'm entering the craft. It's physical **and** nonphysical at the same time, I understand that. It's a projection, but it's very real. I'm in a cubicle in the lower level, off to a side, that has a specialized vibration for earth beings. The being I'm in touch with is clearly nonphysical. It's a nonphysical world, a nonphysical arena of consciousness and knowledge.

Yet my surroundings are of materials, not known to me. They are plastic, but they're not plastic, they're alive! There are layers and layers of lights and passage ways that I can focus on if I choose. It's exciting to realize the technology inherent in the craft, how it merges physical projection with mental attributes . . . so beautifully merged. It's all vibrating and I can focus on any of the vibrations. It can be physically real, or it can be a dream, I have a choice.

It's a mother ship. The mission is to be acquainted with a meeting ground of probabilities. A meeting ground that I can understand, relate to, and accept in physical terms. I'm transfixed by the peach lights as they blink. I'm moving with them into another mental space. . . . Now I'm back. The blue light allows the merging of my energy with the energy of the experience. The peach light carries me through . . . it's an understanding that I can't comprehend in some part. I'm told I don't have to comprehend it now. The peach light is connected to the essence of my totality and merges into a circuit with the blue light. They're both calming, but the blue light keeps me grounded. The peach light takes me on journeys that I'm free to explore.

There are worlds that I am free to entertain but they are beyond my comprehension. I am not ready, but for my enjoyment, they're allowing me to glance. Some are of my future, some are off to the side. Some are closer to the creation itself. There are time warps involved. These worlds are here now, but they're not in my perspective – yet they are in the "moment". It's how I'm entertaining the experience, it's my own illusion.

The Orion energies that are merging these rememberings into my physical focus are one with the experience. There are many worlds to transcend, many worlds to explore. I will explore them at my own pace. I'm being introduced and invited to merge these

3

knowings into an earth perspective that I can relate to . . . in the channeling process that I'm acquiescing to. To them it's not channeling, it's simply opening up to a remembering of who I am and what the planet represents in greater terms . . . how I can now relate to people I come in contact with on a soul level and transcend their ego perspective. It's an initiation into soul.

I had meetings on that craft with representations of different vibrations that I would channel in the future . . . Playing with time, this was a grand meeting place that was orchestrated. Many aspects of my greater self are present, along with different energies that were part of the earth plane (and now interested in "Continuous Energy") . . . In light form, in their own focus with an introduction and a handshake of an agreement that I acquiesced to in this experience . . . and that's another meaning of this gathering.

There's no fear on the mother ship at all. There are beings on the ship that are projecting a physical image, yet they know that they're not physical. They're playing the game of manifesting physically for fun, just as I am doing in the life I left behind on the airplane. They're drawing the similarities to my attention . . . that I, besides reincarnational selves, have connections on other planets. So in one sense, it's simply a reunion . . . a remembering.

I'm seeing other portals of the craft. There are actually environments on the craft that create physical worlds to explore and merge with. There's some confusion as to how they're able to manifest the worlds for their merging . . . I'm told I'm misinterpreting how they're manifesting. They're simply merging their vibration with the (target) worlds. The mother ship is misunderstood. It's not that space ships emerge from the mother ship, as an understanding of thought patterns emerging from the ship. It manifests ships that re-emerge into the time and space of the desired locale. I don't quite understand how they create (these projections). I'm told not to worry about it, just to observe it. And I'm watching them do it. It's amazing!

Their computer onboard is a crystal that they merge with, individually or in a group. It doesn't matter. It's not a computer in our terms, it will do far more than ours. It's somehow the future of our computer technology. The memory is entertained in consciousness – that is simply tucked away in various compartments to be drawn on at a later time. Different compartments of consciousness that are part of the computer spin (around). And in the spinning motion, when one desires to re-acquaint oneself with the vibration that's entertained in the memory, there is a merging process that at first is mental. But it becomes physical in the manifestation of the desired world, if the world is physical. It's all a mind game, with the computer guiding the desire and the intention of the interaction.

The spinning is most fascinating, it's going so fast. There are all kinds of lights attached to the computer. It's like a mushroom. It changes as I stare at it, it's not the same computer that it was a minute ago. Now it's a mushroom shape and it's enclosed in the center of the ship. It's fascinating because it's a merging of physical and nonphysical focus. It's the recognition that my thought can "create" any aspect of the light (programmed in the computer) that I wish to entertain. They understand that so implicitly and they're sharing it with me.

I'm brought back to the cubicle where I started now. And the beings that are walking around, the programmed beings, they're more than that. They're emanations from the consciousness of the being I'm speaking to, that have the freedom to entertain their own focus and their own learning . . . that somehow merges with the being, but yet goes its own way in a manner that I don't understand because it seems mechanical. I don't understand how it can be alive and mechanical at the same time. They walk around in a strange fashion.

It's clear that the one I'm interacting with is the same being I met in Egypt, that I first met in my dreams (several years earlier). The dream experiences were equally valid to the experience that I'm now entertaining, except I forgot most of them (the dreams) upon awakening. I didn't know the significance of the dream introductions. I can look at the physical attributes of the space ship, and I know that I'm privileged to be consciously aware of the technology. I'm very content. I don't want to go back to the planet yet, I want to move on, but I'm not ready and I know that.

I'm awed at the wonderment of this craft. In size, in physical focus, it would be about three miles vertically and about twelve miles in diameter. It's shaped as a sphere that changes shape based on the vibration in which it finds itself. It's totally flexible in shape. From my perspective I would envision it as round, but at the same time not round, having the capacity to take on many shapes. As it moves through dimensions it changes shape. As it de-materializes and re-materializes it changes shapes to the belief structure of the environment in which it finds itself. Where I am right now, it's simply a mental construct that appears to be round. The craft is used by physical beings. The projection is borrowed by the Orion energies for our meeting place, so I can look at it from many different perspectives. It's not just a projection. I'm learning now that it's a physical craft that is utilized by other beings for their own purposes.

I'm being infused with a knowing of the Orion energies that I'm imparting back onto the earth plane. I made an agreement to remember my connectedness to Orion. To teach others that that knowing is available to all. To teach myself to believe in what I'm perceiving. I agreed to remember the initiation of the channeling process that was entertained on that craft. It was left open as to how I would remember the experience, in what timing I would remember it. It was all left open to my intent and how I would deal with it on an ego level."

(end of hypnosis)

● ● ●

When this manuscript began there was the recognition that the following lessons were channeled, but the energy behind these knowings seemed impersonal. By "channeled", I mean that the concepts appeared to come from outside of myself since I had no conscious awareness of "continuous energy". So it happened in September of 1988, almost a year after the initiation of this project, that a more intimate contact with the co-authors was made. It had been through subsequent channelings that I came to understand upcoming earth changes in far more expansive terms.

• • •

The earth shall heal itself. We will learn to appreciate the intricate balances between the earth's awareness of itself, our awareness of ourselves, and the knowing that there is indeed no separation between us and the planet that supports us. We are a part of nature and fit into the scheme of nature's expression. Survival of the fittest has never applied – and through this awareness, we will grow together in ways that will scare some of us, excite some of us, and will assuredly challenge all of us. A threshold has been met where we've collectively reached beyond ourselves scientifically relative to an understanding of our oneness – and the earth itself will shake us free of the limitations we have placed upon our experience.

"Continuous Energy" addresses these issues in the context of earth change – incorporating an understanding of an upcoming vibrational shift that will force us to come to terms with not only the connections we share with our planet, but an energy process that utilizes this knowing in quite practical terms. Through the speeding up and alteration of our brain activity, we will gain an appreciation of this wholeness and grow to love ourselves and understand our divinity. The potential of continuous energy puts into useful perspective that which we are capable of and that which will allow us a framework of "proof" that we are infinitely more than we have been taught to accept in ego terms.

• • •

7

To appreciate how this manuscript evolved, I will hypothetically begin with a search for meaning in my life in the midsixties after a death experience involving an automobile accident. As I lay in that hospital bed wracked in pain and disorientation, I made a promise to myself to find out what was happening to me and to make sense out of a seemingly meaningless universe. Starting with a comparison of various religions, I gradually moved on to read the Eastern philosophies, T. Lobsang Rampa, Edgar Cayce, and finally Jane Roberts' twenty-one books that I will collectively refer to as the "Seth material".

My first exposure to that material was "Seth Speaks" in 1976. I immediately began having psychic experiences that more or less coincided with the concepts I was entertaining at the time. I had various breakthroughs in experiencing and comprehending the material as I learned to "set my ego aside" while assimilating various relaxation techniques of self hypnosis, yoga breathing and psychological time(1). I eventually devised a method of visualizing Seth's levels of consciousness(2) while in psychological time and would simply suggest experiences at any given level. Gradually, I learned how to break down barriers of time and space, communicate with the trees and view nature as an extension of myself.

There was no accompanying fear with regard to these altered states with the exception of the extreme disorientation that began with my death experience in 1964 – that would re-occur sporadically over the next fifteen years. This later became understood as the activation of my cellular memory, involving a perception of past, present and future events on the part of my cells "all at once". Understanding that a cell has no ego to contend with, it perceives no time or space limitations and knows of its simultaneous existences. This translated into a sensation of massiveness on the part of my physical body, during which time I would be unable to discern spatial relationships. The panic that always accompanied these events finally evolved into a sense of being able to control this awareness and enjoy the gateway it provided into other dimensions.

My psychic explorations continued with an odyssey of many out-of-body experiences that led me through tunnel like warps into alien worlds, some physical and some not. Some where light and sound were present and some where one or the other seemed to be absent. There were realities that were geometric patterns or musical constructions, and many that seemed completely untranslatable. What struck me about these experiences was the infinite number of perspectives there are and the infinite variety of values to be explored. I believe that it was this obsession with "relative perception" that ultimately led to the orchestration of this book.

The manuscript itself began with a telephone conversation with Beth Karish on 11-2-87. Beth and I had met briefly at the Munedowk Retreat Center in Kiel, Wisconsin where I had given a talk on "My Awareness of Being a Walk-in and the Psychic Experiences that Followed" (subject matter of a future book). Beth later asked me if I would give a similar presentation at her Windows of Light book store in Appleton, Wisconsin. Around that time, we visited her friend Anna May Cottrell's house, where weekly gatherings were taking place during which time Anna May would channel her guides and somehow direct a group of ten or so people through an out-of-body experience that would mesh with the subject matter of her channeling.

On the telephone conversation in question, Beth had been discussing her most recent visit with Anna May's group and was describing an out-of-body experience she had in which she found herself "outlining the pattern of her intended manifestation" and somehow filling it in with her own psychic energy. I found her description overwhelmingly familiar and while on the telephone, spontaneously "bilocated" to find myself floating in space and merged quite joyously with her soul energy. I had encountered several bilocation experiences previously, but I had never merged with anyone in quite this manner. I had been describing these happenings to Beth all along and when I finished, she suggested I hang up the telephone and write down my interpretation of these events and ask my guides for further insights.

The following notes of that experience evolved into an automatic writing format that provided me with an introduction to "Continuous Energy". It begins with my own notes and proceeds to an understanding that I am channeling – as indicated by messages being directed "to" me . . .

Telephone conversation with Beth Karish 11-2-87:

[Michael: "I felt Beth's soul energy as one with mine in a most remarkable way. We were engaged in a union as you might visualize a physical relationship, except now I was part of her soul energy and she part of mine. We shared a multidimensional closeness with boundaries unknown to the planet at this time. It was as if we were of the same soul essence, joined for purposes of similar intent in the understanding and transmutation of an energy force into this time and space – so powerful and so revolutionary, that it will change the physics of our awareness. There is in our cellular memory an energy of thought-form and projection as it outlines the pattern of our intended manifestation, that creates an instantaneous and simultaneous creation of a greater energy mass than was previously understood or conceived. This power at our disposal will be used to re-create artifacts of antiquity in a way that will **reveal lost abilities of energy transformation.**

[Channeled: This can of course be used in unproductive ways, but this was a lesson of the past "you" will not repeat on your planet at this time. You and Beth were a part of the priesthood of Balzerious, on Atlantis, and had privilege and honor because of your abilities of putting into practical application that which we are introducing to you. Your challenge is to expand your intellectual **and** intuitive abilities – to remember and bring to the forefront these "lost sciences". The time is right, and a pattern of similar intent and cohesiveness had to be established on your planet to get the ball rolling. The direction that these revelations will take will surprise not only your physicists, but your esoteric and religious scholars as well. Psychic memories will come to the surface within many individuals to form a cohesive front for further advances that will help **carry you into a new age**. Do not be intimidated by the awesome responsibility you feel, for you had agreed to do this before you took physical form. We suggest you take a break and prepare for "Lesson One" at a later time.

[Michael: While Beth and I were on the telephone, I felt that we were floating in space making love – but making love as a union of souls merging in a way quite unknown, multidimensional and orgasmic in an utterly spectacular way. [Channeled: This implied a love far more expansive than is usually assigned to the word. This implied an explosion and implosion of "All That Is" to form the boundary of your experience in a manner quite expansive relative to your norm of love making and shared feelings. Here, your feelings went beyond the mental and beyond the emotional (as you understand them), to encompass the love of "All That Is" in a way that seemed quite personalized between two individuals. You felt as though you were floating because you couldn't visualize the act as a physical process.

[Michael: I also felt an energy too powerful for our planet to assimilate. It was as though it was just **waiting at the gates of our awareness**, to be introduced by an earthling as an old friend might introduce you to his loving mate. [Channeled: Old friends in a reunion, not to be feared, but instead welcomed as an alchemist mixes his potion in a loving blending to create "eternal life" – for you are entering into an age of eternal perspective, far outpacing your current concepts of calendar time."

• • •

In retrospect then, the initiation of this book does make sense given my long-standing obsession with the Seth material and my particular focus on the illusionary aspects of our physical perspective. In October of 1987, shortly before this book began, I was at a conference in Ottawa, Canada sponsored by my friend Serge Grandbois. During that conference Serge channeled several energies, including "Anderson", who is one of the main energies behind this book. Anderson can be described as a "traveler", a nonphysical group energy that travels through dimensions imparting awarenesses that the reality in question is open to receiving – that in our case will help move us into an understanding of "continuous energy". Several discussions with Anderson dealt with Einstein's theory of relativity and how it deals with energy and matter.

To my surprise, within a few short months of that conference, I found myself "taking dictation" on the nature of thought, continuous energy, and upcoming earth changes. This manuscript then, will serve as a primer to the understanding of a self-generating energy process and a feel for our "connectedness" that makes this system possible.

● ● ●

Perhaps a bit of page hopping will serve you in introducing some of the complexities of "Continuous Energy". There are many concepts being introduced that may seem quite strange, so please maintain an open mind. The first few lessons came about rather abruptly, but given a chance, the book will begin to flow. The manuscript is simple enough to grasp overall, yet difficult enough to challenge you to your limits.

● ● ●

(1) PSYCHOLOGICAL TIME:

Psychological time is one of the numerous inner senses mentioned in the "Seth Material". It represents an altered state that can easily be reached by relaxation and the clearing of extraneous thought. It was originally intended as a meeting ground of the inner worlds of the mind and the seeming outer worlds of experience[1] – when man was experimenting with ego development many thousands of years ago.

I've always considered psychological time as a space I can reach mentally by expanding my "inner vision". It always feels like I am outside of time and free of ego restraints, and from that perspective able to access various altered states by mere suggestion.

1- "The Seth Material" by Jane Roberts. Chapter 19

(2) LEVELS OF CONSCIOUSNESS:

Levels of consciousness are closely related to the various inner senses referenced above. An understanding of the inner senses reveal alternate perceptive abilities that are available by looking inwardly as opposed to utilizing outer physical senses such as our eyes, ears, touch etc. Our inner senses "prove" beyond any doubt the roots of our existence outside of time and space. The Seth material identified nine inner senses[1] (or levels of consciousness) which I was able to experience to a large degree. I began by "objectifying" them on a schematic chart for purposes of identifying them while in psychological time and simply suggesting experiences at any given level, i.e. reincarnational insights, alternate realities, alpha levels for purposes of healing, various means of merging my awareness with other life forms, etc.

1- "Seth Speaks" by Jane Roberts. Chapter 19, Session 574

"The manuscript is simple enough to grasp overall, yet difficult enough to challenge you to your limits."

"Unleashing of this energy through understanding & direction are the key ingredients."

Chapter One

COORDINATE POINTS & PROJECTION

LESSON (1), NOVEMBER 3, 1987

As we stated earlier, the time is ripe for the implementation of a new thought-form pattern of energy development compatible with your planet's inner knowing – but not necessarily compatible with your current laws of physics. We are most interested in the **preservation of your planet's atmosphere,** as interstellar space is interconnected and could be contaminated with the narrow-minded usage of the tools at your disposal(1). We see fit to blend into your awareness a timesaving perspective that can be harnessed for use as a propellant to nurture your physical constructions with far less effort and energy. Transport will be considered at a later time. First master the basics as presented into your time frame.

All the necessary components for the introduction of these energies are available to you at this time. All that is needed is an understanding of the thought process required to harness this procedure. As we proceed, your cellular memory will provide bridges to understanding that will eventually yield a cohesive package of easy to follow steps. Understand that you will have a model of "All That Is" – idea construction forming matter, and simultaneous probabilities "unforming antimatter". Finite resources may at some point appear to limit your creative process, but what is lacking in materials can be replicated by utilizing coordinate points(2) at designated angles. We will enhance your concepts of engineering to cosmic proportions, in a way most enjoyable and rewarding to the best of your architects and consulting engineers. End of Lesson One.

COMMENT:

Many of the footnotes that follow in this and subsequent lessons will deal with concepts I first became aware of in the "Seth material" – the term I use loosely to reference the collection of books written by the late Jane Roberts and her husband Robert Butts[1]. In many respects, this manuscript will review those concepts, and in fact depend on them for an understanding of the energy system "we" are about to unravel. In other respects, we will expand on those thoughts and move into territory not yet explored in scientific or metaphysical writings.

1 – Aside from the creative genius of Jane Roberts, the Seth material would probably never have been published had it not been for the patience and dedication of Robert Butts. Rob meticulously and accurately utilized his own brand of shorthand to transcribe all of the channeled portions of Jane's manuscripts.

What makes the collection of these books so outstanding is the sheer scope and clarity of the information. Had it not been for Mr. Butt's thousands of hours of note taking, we simply would not have the plethora of material that **is** so readily available.

(1) QUESTION:

Given the illusionary aspects of our plane, how can we affect other star systems that exhibit a different vibrational frequency? It is my understanding that our plane is a relatively isolated one in that we are more or less in a soundproof room.

Your means of warfare, particularly your atomic warheads, could have a profound impact on interstellar space in ways that escape your understanding. Let it suffice to say that other star systems in relative proximity to your vibrational patterns would be affected in a manner that toys with what could open the doors to certain models of probable destruction.

(2) COORDINATE POINTS:

Coordinate points are described as "points of double reality", where realities coincide or merge. This has to be understood in the context of realizing the illusionary aspects of space, where literally an infinite number of conscious perspectives exist within the very space we consider our own, i.e. the room in which we find ourselves. The Seth material identified four major coordinate points that intersect all realities, seen as "channels through which energy flows", as well as a vast number of less intense channels[1]. When any of our thoughts or emotions reaches a certain intensity, they would attract the power of one of these points.

This manuscript will expand on these thoughts and build up to an understanding that coordinate point activity is the very process of how we create and maintain the continuous thrust of our physical reality.

1- "Seth Speaks" by Jane Roberts. Chapter 5, Session 524

• • •

LESSON (2), NOVEMBER 4, 1987

Idea construction(1) is the concept of creation that you understand as **projection**(2). Projection is only part of the process we wish to decipher for your linear   understanding. Although projection may seem meaningless or "empty" to you, it involves the implied essence of "All That Is" in every projection, whether perceived by your physical senses or not - or whether seemingly physical from our perspective or not. So understand that projection is as "real" as any thought, or any physical object from your perspective. Therefore, your understanding needs refining in terms of validity. Know that your interstellar space can indeed affect other systems around your earth in a way most direct by even the least of your imaginings. We wish to imply the **sacredness of all space,** whether "illusion" in your terms or not. This does not imply the same concentration of energy in all projections, but it does imply the same principle.

17

Therefore, when you project your thoughts into a desired manifestation, do so with the understanding that your projections are filled with the same essence as your precious brain that emits the message. This may empower the sense of your creative abilities in a way we wish to explore with you. Know also, that the intensity of your projection in terms of its concentration and "knowing" of its simultaneous result, play an important role in the process. When we are finished, you will have the ability to project your essence of an outline of that which you intend to manifest or transport in a way most proficient by standards even your Atlantian self will marvel at.

(1) IDEA CONSTRUCTION:

In September of 1963, Jane Roberts had an out-of-body experience during which time she utilized automatic writing to create the manuscript known as "The Physical Universe as Idea Construction". Portions of that work can be found in Chapter One of "The Seth Material". The information contained in that first breakthrough is closely related to the gist of the many books that would follow.

The concept of Idea Construction describes the process by which we translate our psychic energy into ideas that are then projected outwardly and interpreted as our physical world. Understanding the thoughts contained in those pages directs us to the awareness that **we are creators,** and that we not only create own subjective experience, but that we also have a hand in creating the physical universe itself.

(2) PROJECTION:

An insight into the illusionary aspects of our physical plane becomes a prerequisite to the understanding of "continuous energy". Our physical world is an **illusion** to the perspective of an energy/personality outside of our vibration, yet very real to us as sensed by our physical focus.

Our inner self emits energy on a subconscious level that continually creates and forms the physical objects that are "then" perceived as real or solid – but they are real only through the guise of our physical senses. Each individual creates his or her own physical object that becomes his or her own "projection". Others create "their" own physical objects (and perspective) in like manner – and we telepathically agree on the placement of those objects. If ten individuals are observing the "same" table, there are then ten tables – each being a personalized projection being created by every person taking part in this "shared projection".

Carrying this understanding further, our entire physical planet becomes a "mass projection" and an illusion to those perspectives outside of our vibration – but very real to us who choose to take part in this reality. Try to sense the connection here between "idea construction" and the manner in which we create our illusionary environment.

My previous understanding of the "illusion" was that since our world is only a projection, it was a "benign projection" that couldn't possibly have an impact on any reality outside of our range or frequency of vibration. This lesson begins to clarify the power of projection and hence the power of visualization, which becomes a necessary acknowledgement in the unraveling of continuous energy.

● ● ●

LESSON (3), NOVEMBER 4, 1987

As time relates to space there is a seeming gestalt(1) as you might understand it – but it implies something intensely more vital, more of the essence of All That Is as it imparts value fulfillment and potentials onto each of these coordinate points (of space/time). Some of these points are simply a bit more concentrated than others, packaged in a way that would seem to your instruments to alter the gravitational pull of the moon a bit more or less than the "space" next to it. As you move along the scale of coordinate points, all the way "up" to your major points (in Sethian terms), you have a profound power station of sorts that refuels your system with renewed bursts of energy. All systems are open, one to another, so in effect you are feeding each other in a most harmonious way. Therefore, you aren't really being resupplied from "outside" of your system.

Space is more of an attribute of thought than a measure of distance. There can be what appears to be a folding effect of space as it joins into arrangements with other cooperative ventures of seeming space – but again, it is an attribute of thought. Know that the coordinate points you will be dealing with in the practical application of these concepts will be of the intermediate range in terms of intensity. Biologically, you are not equipped to assimilate power sources that you could term beyond your voltage capacity. We are not speaking in electrical terms as you would normally understand it, but in terms of assimilating energies for transmutation into designated ends.

COMMENT:

I have been toying with the connectedness of time and space for many years, as to how they entertain one another. The day after dictating this session, I had been contemplating this issue and momentarily came to the conclusion that time (or the "eternal now") somehow had more validity than space, since space was completely an illusion. Between Lessons 3 and 4, I came up with the following response:

As to your earlier conclusion that time is of the only real essence since space is more of an illusion than time, or the eternal now, know that time and space both entertain one another quite symbiotically to help form the grid work of the physical universe. And when discussed in conjunction with the concept of a vibration unique to each space/time coordinate, you have a more complete explanation of the model toward which we wish you to understand and develop an emotional relationship.

(1) GESTALTS:

A gestalt basically refers to the understanding that all aspects of reality are correlated, connected and one, with no inherent boundaries. Events can be artificially grouped into seeming patterns or gestalts within the connectedness of All That Is – yet the universe is one overriding pattern that is "happening" at once.

20

Gestalt thinking acknowledges this connectedness in repudiating the seeming randomness of behavior, events or phenomena. It becomes evident that all seeming boundaries or separations are but smaller pictures of a particular gestalt where missing links (or thought patterns) have us believing in the separation of one event from another. Upon further examination, we discover the wider relationship understanding of the chosen issue.

The dictionary defines a gestalt as . . . "a physical or psychological configuration so unified as a whole that its properties cannot be derived from its parts[1]". We can set up any number of arbitrary groupings or boundaries and consider them a gestalt. In this context, it becomes simply a pattern of focus and concentration that we choose to deal with for a particular relationship understanding – as we move into an ever grander perspective of self.

An example of a gestalt would be our physical body where each atom contains its own individual awareness – and at the same time joins with other atoms to form molecules. Molecules in like-manner do the same to form organs and bone structure, which in turn create the total body awareness. The body gestalt, then, allows even the individual atom the ability to maintain its independence while it expresses itself and shares with the overall body perspective. This level of expression would not be possible without joining in this pooling of consciousness. And the magic of gestalts is that the greater awareness becomes infinitely more than the sum of the individual parts.

It was this initial understanding that led me to believe in an endless configuration of further out gestalts. I pictured the various body parts as combining consciousness to help create our identity, and our identities joining in like-manner to orchestrate a soul perspective. It seemed logical to carry this analogy further and envision a grouping of souls into yet another gestalt and the grouping of oversouls into still another.

In June of 1987, while Serge Grandbois was channeling "Anderson"[2] for my benefit, it was pointed out that I was searching for an ever expanding outward continuation of gestalts. Realizing in that moment that I was looking for a "beyond", it struck me that the whole notion of beyond is limiting and that it is far more accurate to think in terms of an "eternal now and constant creation". Gestalts had to be seen as having no beginning, end, or beyond.

It also began to make sense that through a soul's evolution, a point is reached where the ego is transcended and the illusion of the separation is acknowledged. This in turn breaks down all fear in the embrace of our oneness.

1- "The American Heritage Dictionary", second college edition, p.556

2- **Anderson** was identified in the introduction as one of the main energies behind the orchestration of this manuscript. "He" is channeled by Serge Grandbois who resides in Ottawa, Canada. Aside from being a friend, Serge's channeling is among the most far reaching that I have ever encountered.

● ● ●

LESSON (4), NOVEMBER 5, 1987

The reproductive cycle of your species involves a multidimensional interchange of psychological intent interspliced with matter to form the nucleus of an embryo. This process takes place outside of time, but inside a vortex of energy you would consider matter. Here, time and space are intricately manipulated for the purpose of introducing a pattern to be followed for the intent of the consciousness involved. This pattern can be considered an outline or blueprint of not only physical form, but mental and emotional factors that will interact with the emerging personality.

Likewise, an outline of form that you wish to **materialize** starts with a process that takes place outside of time. And through your intent(1) and focus, you propel your energy into this designated pattern in a way that impinges into your time - as well as a simultaneously creative reproductive process into parallel dimensions. Your focus allows only a one-dimensional perspective, but rest assured that all aspects of your "self" are affected - whether consciously recognized or not, in a gestalt of interaction that in total involves a creative thrust beyond what you would consider even your soul boundaries.

We are expanding your sense of boundaries here to give you a **feel for the creative process** as it impinges on a far greater expanse of time and space than you currently imagine. Likewise, creations and creativity from "other" systems impinge into your system, usually unnoticed by your physical senses, but open to your intuitive knowing. This is relevant only in giving you an appreciation for the far reaching thrust of creativity at your disposal.

(1) INTENT:

Relative to common usage, intent simply implies concentration toward a particular focus. In the context of this manuscript and an understanding of continuous energy, intent takes on an infinitely richer connotation. It becomes all inclusive with regard to belief, ideal, expression and direction. It becomes immersed in an understanding of our divinity and power of being that makes the essence of our thought the very essence of All That Is.

• • •

LESSON (5), NOVEMBER 6, 1987

Thus far we have been supplying you with an outline of the creative process as you relate it to the physical reality you are now part of. Realize also that this process implies all other realities, physical and otherwise. The process itself is what is important – as it is replicated in other systems for the **root assumptions(1)** involved. This process can be most useful on your plane as a source of power that would **eliminate the need for fossil fuels and your atomic energy.** Understand that this power source is already inherent and implied in your current technology as it impinges onto your psychological reality and personhood. What is needed is a change of focus from the concept of a power supply outside of yourselves – to one quite immersed in your cells already.

23

Unleashing of this energy through **understanding and direction** are the key ingredients. Through mental process, you are quite capable on individual levels of manifesting your needs in a physical way – and in total, your societies are more than able to energize your cities using a simple technique of coordinate point manipulation to unharness a power supply that will meet all of your demands. This unleashing involves a preliminary understanding of the physics of matter as it relates to thought, and the power of thought when used in a directed manner.

(1) ROOT ASSUMPTIONS:

Every perspective, whether in physical terms or not, makes certain assumptions relative to the parameters of its chosen experience. This is closely aligned with the notion of "camouflage" discussed in Lesson 64. The root assumptions of our plane would all combine to represent our particular camouflage that we in turn accept as the focus of our reality, i.e. time and space, a physical perspective etc.

● ● ●

LESSON (6), NOVEMBER 7, 1987

The power of thought, as you understand it, is but a smattering of All That Is in capsule form. The physical world seen as a projection should imply the power of thought when connected to your psychic energy, that indeed creates your physical form. When looked at in this vein, you can see that your thoughts are **the building blocks of matter** – from a perspective quiteoutside of matter. Now think of this vast vortex of energy, outside of matter, that powers your thoughts in the first place. Here, there is a cohesive blending of time and space through your coordinate points, into a picture of reality that you hold as "real". You can utilize the same process of directing this energy to formulate a "pre-matter" consideration that can then be triggered into full manifestation as you solidify your intention.

Think in terms of steps, as you would build bridges to connect one land mass to another. Except here, your bridges are connecting one thought pattern to another. The end result will be most startling when you consider that you have created an object of physical appearance from the building blocks of thought. As you start to consider thought as your most prized possession(1), realize that you have much discretion in the utilization and direction of this thought as it impinges into your time and space. Used in a directed manner, it can be most powerful in any terms you wish to consider.

(1) THOUGHT:

"Thinking" becomes possible on our plane only because our vibration is slow enough to distinguish between our thoughts and the result of our thoughts – hence we are able to consider cause and effect an attribute of our reality. In a plane where the vibration is noticeably faster, there would be no such gap – but rather some form of direct cognition and instant materialization.

● ● ●

LESSON (7), NOVEMBER 8, 1987

The predominate blockage preventing an understanding of our energy source is **your system of belief.** It has evolved through your industrial revolution into a rather dogmatic perspective of separate domain of science, religion and nature – not seeing yourselves as part of nature, and not understanding that your science and religion are by-products of your need to feel separate from All That Is in a way that is quite unnecessary(1). When you approach your science with the love implied in All That Is as impressed in your person-hood and physical reality, you will sense on an intuitive level the power of this love as it finds its way into your reality. This love, or universal energy, can be tapped as you might consider a "faucet of being", rather directly from your consciousness into your physical plane. As trite as this might sound, it is indeed the case. For you also have the belief that you need elaborate apparatus or electronic gear to access "power" on your plane.

25

(1) ON DUALITIES & MERGING WITH A FLOWER:

The concept of separation and dualities had always confused me in the context of reading Eastern philosophy. I eventually came to understand that we are not separate from our environment as a result of numerous altered states that acted as "proof" of my connectedness. One of my most enjoyable experiences leading to a sense of oneness involved the merging of my consciousness with a rose. This experience occurred quite spontaneously in October of 1981 and offered me the following perspective – taken from notes transcribed immediately afterwards:

. . . There was a sudden awareness of its aura and sensed oneness with the earth, trees and other plants. It exuded a "sureness" of its perfect right to exist and express itself – while at the same time undergoing a fascinating transformation of energy in the continuous creation of its physical image, having an awareness of the entire process. From the focus of a cell on its stem, the flower was a universe to behold. And from its overall knowing of itself, it was an oversoul of major significance.

The rose, operating without an ego, had a simultaneous sense of past, present and future – of its death and total realignment of its atoms while still maintaining its identity of a rose. Its self-conception was anything but a physical object from our perspective, yet the richness of its knowing transcended any need to understand our interpretation of its image. Most apparent was a fascinating sense of unity and cooperation among various aspects of its energy as it sensed its support from the soil underneath, recognizing that it also supported the soil. And within this oneness, there was a knowing of its placement on the planet as part of the continuum it felt with all other flowers and trees, soil and rock, air and sea. It saw no separation with its environment while knowing itself as an expression of pure exuberance that "knows" the underlying thrust of unconditional love.

● ● ●

LESSON (8), NOVEMBER 8, 1987

In the simplest of terms, you have the capacity to energize your bodies, your vehicles and your cities in an effortless manner – once understood. The prerequisite here, as already stated, is a re-arranging of your thought processes and beliefs from a source outside of yourselves to one contained in your creaturehood. This will be accomplished quite spontaneously when you reach the threshold of understanding and practice necessary to observe initial results. The practice involved is one of **concentration and direction** of "All That Is", through your subconscious, into your cellular memory and translated into your awareness through a knowing that will be triggered by prior knowledge and experience in these techniques. We are providing you with a background first, for your edification, so as to make the "system" workable in the context of your beliefs revolving around who and what you are.

Understand that your bodies, and the consciousness that forms them, are none other than "All That Is" in disguise – as in your Halloween just celebrated. And when you take off your masks, you will find the power within quite amazing and capable of that which we are outlining for you. And beyond that, you will see that you have an even greater power source at your disposal, to be integrated into your awareness and identity – to eventually eliminate the need for competition and wars. Once you sense that you are all gods in disguise, you will find it quite useless to kill one another since you will realize that the "other" (or object of your malice), is yet another aspect of yourselves. The energy that we speak of is but an attribute of All That Is in useful form, to not only power your vehicles and light your cities, but also available to all in equal proportion. Once understood, there will be a unity on your planet in the awakening of this awareness. You will all rejoice in your oneness with each other and the energy that unites you – and the knowing of the source of this love.

QUESTION:

What is the source of these lessons?

The source of these writings is not as important as the messages we give you. If you must have an identity behind these concepts, let it be "All That Is" imparting knowledge to you in a way that you will understand it. To break down "All That Is" into identifiable form that will appease you, we are a group energy of formless worlds interested in your progress as a people into an age that will eliminate the need for competitive infighting between nations for the natural resources in and on your planet. There is enough energy for all – if you learn how to approach the issue from the perspective of a source within yourselves. It is that simple, although it will take some re-arranging of your thought concepts to appreciate the simplicity.

Chapter Two

MANIFESTATION

LESSON (9), NOVEMBER 9, 1987

Understanding the **process of manifestation** from a physical perspective requires a concentrated focus on that which you intend. Starting from a basic knowing of what you intend, project outwardly an outline in "dot-matrix" format, as in your computer printer style of type. Then, to the best of your ability, simply fill in the outline with as much emotional impact as you can - believing the entire time that that which you are materializing is yours in the moment. Sense the aura around the "object" and the flow of "All That Is" from your end of the **circuit** to the outline itself and back again, as in a completed electrical schematic.

Know that this process implies more than an exercise in visualization and that you are indeed creating a model with "authentic" building blocks, quite as valid as will the end result contain. To the extent that your intent is clear and your "circuit" has been completed, the pre-formulated schematic will build up energy and momentum to finally emerge into your system. The method of entry may appear under ordinary guise of happenstance, but what you have actually accomplished is the manipulation of **Framework-II(1)** and the bending of universal intent in your direction.

The abilities of your consciousness to master this procedure will require practice, as in any skill - but know that through continued application you will sharpen your abilities, which in turn will lead to other applications (of the creative principle) into areas quite outside of your current physical laws. The process itself will evolve into a continuous refinement for each application and desired end. We suggest you begin practicing on relatively simple ends and have your successes build up, one after the other, so as to enhance your confidence which will greatly expand your overall approach. Ultimately, only your creativity and imagination will limit your objectives.

(1) FRAMEWORK-II:

In Sethian terms, Framework-I would be our everyday world of appearance and perspective of physical focus. Framework-II becomes the inner psychological medium that supports the outer world – in one context as a vast communication network through which all aspects of our planet keep in touch. Whatever it takes to help orchestrate an event is organized in Framework-II. Coincidences, accidental meetings, or just being at the right place at the right time. All the details are worked out here to bring about the desired event[1]. This medium can be worked with in visualization terms to manifest a desired outcome.

1- "The Individual and The Nature Of Mass Events" - A Seth Book by Jane Roberts. Chapter 2, Session 815

● ● ●

LESSON (10), NOVEMBER 10, 1987

Creating that which you desire needs some clarification in your own mind as to what you truly desire. For the distinction between what you think you desire – and what you believe and expect, can have a far greater impact on your probable future than you realize. If you truly define that which you desire, in all the ramifications of the trade-offs involved, you may be rather surprised to discover that you really don't want what you think you desire. Fear, feelings of worthlessness, and simply a belief that it is not obtainable can all stand in your way. So the clearer your desire, the faster the manifestation process will trigger the event in your reality and time frame.

To simplify the procedure (desire and manifestation), write down clearly what you intend and note any and all objections to the creating of your desire. It is important to truly believe your intent as you do this exercise (simply for this time). So make it a playful experience, believing for the moment that you have what you want. Now what comes into your awareness? This can be feelings of joy, or blocks to the manifestation process that you will have to deal with. These beliefs, or fears that will momentarily take you off your status quo, must be addressed. Realize simply that all **change** implies some possible temporary discomfort, but that it is indeed temporary – and if not for change, you can not grow into more of that which you are capable of becoming.

• • •

LESSON (11), NOVEMBER 11, 1987

The approach taken toward **defining your desire** doesn't have to be a complicated procedure, but rather an honest one – dealing with the trade-offs implied. These trade-offs involve necessary changes that your desire would bring into your daily reality and experience. To deny the anxiety of these changes can greatly inhibit the process. Therefore, an open and positive attitude greatly facilitates that desired event you have visualized. Know that you are getting support from other aspects of yourself in ways you might not appreciate at the time, and instead sense only the anxiety from ego levels of your personality.

All levels of yourself are valid, and so must be dealt with. Here again, the idea of **expanding your ego**(1) to accommodate a larger sense of self can be integrated into the process in a most invigorating and expansive way. Be especially open to your emotional self in a clear manner, i.e. your dreams, inspirations and flashes, brief as they might be.

Catch glimpses of your **future self**(2) enjoying the spoils of your present efforts. If you can capture the joy of accomplishment of this "future self", you can carry that back with you into your present and integrate the two into a process that will carry your visualization exercise much "deeper" into your psyche for a more vivid and spontaneous occurrence of change. Probabilities here can literally change with blinding speed and impinge into your time frame immediately in your terms. What you are actually accomplishing is a conscious manipulation of time, bringing your future into your present in a most direct way that solidifies your thoughts into an immediately observable process. Your "proof" becomes unmistakable, which adds confidence toward the further expansion of these principles.

QUESTION:

Are there distortions involved in these lessons?

We suggest you keep a perspective on your total project. Know that you are embarking on a major discovery (in scientific terms) of that which your physicists will consider **neutron implosion(3)** – which in effect involves the manipulation of coordinate points to affect surrounding space in a field of energy screens that will enable your scientists to move large blocks of physical matter with the slightest of energy input. Let this be a teaser to your continued efforts and know that we are most excited to proceed!

(1) EXPANSION OF EGO:

When I began my psychic explorations in the midseventies, a sensed loss of identity and apprehension would create an end to my altered state. I found myself very open to suggestion and altered states, but my ego would get in my way and I would fear an infusion of unknown stimuli. This created an instant stalemate – and so a solution had to be found.

Eventually, I devised a technique of moving my ego aside and convincing it that it could grow right along with me in an expansion of consciousness. I created a game whereby I would "objectify" my ego, seemingly separate it from myself, place it in front of me, and carry on a conversation as though it were a different person. "We" would carry on various discussions during which time I would allow my ego to express its protests and fears, and I in turn would assure it that it was not being trampled upon and would actually enjoy the expanded perceptions. After a few "conversations", it became apparent that this procedure was satisfactory and no further problems arose.

(2) FUTURE SELF:

The whole area of communication with this "future self" is explored in a most enjoyable book channeled by my friend Jeff King[1].

1- "Creating Your Success Reality, Practical Application of The Future Self Concept - A Teach Book" by Jeff King. If interested, you can obtain a copy of Jeff's book by mailing $8.00 to Jeffco, P.O. Box 117140, Carrollton, Tx. 75011-7140. (The $8.00 includes postage & handling)

(3) NEUTRON IMPLOSION:

The "process" of neutron implosion becomes a key element in the understanding of continuous energy. It involves the mental or mechanical interaction with the atomic structure of a chosen physical object and the subsequent collapse of the neutron – which in turn leads to the release of an enormous energy potential. There will be much explanation given in later lessons, with the introductory mention at this juncture meant simply as a "teaser" for my benefit.

**"Your entire physical
field is a projection."**

Chapter Three

IMPLOSION

LESSON (12), NOVEMBER 12, 1987

The understanding of physics on your plane has thus far been limited to the physical senses providing "proof" of the molecular structure of matter and the continuous microscopic examination of ever tinier particles, hoping to lead you to the "building block" of all matter. As you know, the only building block is thought(1) – and until that issue is understood, your scientists will go around in circles. There has been considerable progress on your plane with regard to scientific discovery and the ease of living it has produced in some instances – and the potential is there for substantial improvement in some of these conveniences.

You will reach a point of understanding, however, where your linear thinking, especially your constant categorization(2), will take you no further. At this point, you will be forced to admit a gap in your theories and accept the fact that **consciousness is capable of far greater input** into the manipulation of matter than you have cared to admit. Carrying this analogy further, you will be led to the understanding that not only can consciousness affect matter, but it creates matter, dissolves matter, and can move matter in ways thought thoroughly preposterous.

Breakthroughs in understanding will occur when demonstrations can be utilized in controlled experiments – the only seeming proof of value to you at this time. This writing will enable interested readers to demonstrate these concepts to a point and indeed ignite the interest of some very skeptical scientists. Continued experimentation taking some persistence may be necessary – after which there will be unmistakable "proof" of the theories we are expounding. Momentum will build until large budgets will be provided for further experimentation – possibly suited for military purposes, but do not be concerned at the potential weaponry that could result.

(1) COMMENT:

The concept of "idea construction" was introduced in Lesson 2, the gist of which incorporates an understanding of our entire physical universe as a psychic projection that our physical senses interpret as reality. Hence, the only building block of matter in our reality becomes thought[1] – or a collective "idea" that in our case incorporates the intention of a physical focus. In other nonphysical realities, idea construction is still valid, but it would not translate into a solid appearing world. There is a literal infinity of "value fulfillment" in which to explore, with no need for a physical perspective such as ours or a vibration slow enough to necessarily distinguish between an idea and its manifestation.

1- Around the time I dictated these notes, I asked why there was constant reference to "thought" as the building block of the universe, when there reaches a vibrational level where thought is no longer an issue.

"We utilize the concept of thought for your understanding and edification. It is true that we don't deal with thoughts as such, but more with what you would consider ideas and intent. We have a simultaneous sense of the direction and scope our ideas will encapsulate – and also the parallel dimensions that will make use of our constructions. Whereas your thought is translated into physical expression, our ideas are translated into light and vibrational values. To keep matters simple, we will continue to respect your root assumptions and refer to "thought" as the building block of your universe.

(2) CONSTANT CATEGORIZATION:

Since the industrial revolution and the advent of science as the end-all and catalyst of the "modern age", there has been an obsession with constant categorization in many objective disciplines. This has proven to be a mixed blessing, since this approach ignores the basic knowing that the origins of physical reality lie in non-physical realms. Without this appreciation for the richness of creativity, we find ourselves hung up on immortality, origins, and getting to the building blocks of the universe. Huge sums of money are being considered for more and more sophisticated apparatus to unravel these mysteries, where the answers lie in the very understanding of consciousness.

(3) COMMENT:

I had a dream the night of this channeling that offered the insight . . . Once we are able see through the illusion of our physical reality, it's not so difficult to create "additional illusion" in the form of manifestation.

● ● ●

LESSON (13), NOVEMBER 14, 1987

The formless worlds we inhabit are every bit as vital as the physical structures you so believe in. We manipulate through our pathways in a more direct manner because of our understanding of the power of thought. The manner in which we direct our thought is a totally conscious process compared to your species, although this is the direction in which you are moving. We have energy patterns that are invisible to us, but through other senses we have developed, they are quite as apparent as anything on your plane. Our objective here is to **bridge this gap between your thinking process and ours** so as to make the creative process that much clearer, and the matter of energy transformation a natural by-product of that process.

All thought is energy, and all energy is available to "All That Is" in all of its manifestations in equal disbursements – although not in equal concentrations. This comes through awareness of certain quirks(1) in group patterns that are untranslatable at this time. As we proceed with these lessons, you will be able to appreciate and develop a feel for these quirks and break the translation barrier in a way we are unable to do at this point. We are not omnipotent, but relatively more advanced in several areas of concern to you currently. It is our pleasure to share our perspective with you on these matters and grow along with you in this sharing process. As we proceed, we will introduce ourselves in a more personal way – but for now, let us be your unknown but loving counterparts.

(1) QUIRKS:
Quirks are understood to be certain folds of energy, or energy screens, that can be generated and directed by conscious intent. They are explained in Lessons 62 and 67, but could not readily be understood at this juncture without some intermediary material being introduced first.

• • •

LESSON (14), NOVEMBER 14, 1987
The implosion of the neutron analogy given earlier is the best description of the process we will approach in terms you will relate to. Your understanding of coordinate points is in Sethian terms – and you (Michael) have indeed utilized this concept in "healing" energies through visualization on yourself and others(1). We will discuss the subject in terms of implosion first, because coordinate points would be more difficult to explain at this juncture. We will eventually blend in discussions to include coordinate point angles and manipulation – but first, on to basics. We would suggest glancing at a physics overview text, but not until we supply you with concepts you won't find in the conventional sense. The subatomic particles your scientists are now discovering would only confuse the approach we will take.

Implosion, as the word sounds, involves the collapse of a particle, but with an energy source usually considered outside of the affected mass. We will approach implosion as a process that can easily be achieved through thought-form, visualization, and directed energy of latent portions of your mind – that until now have been rendered useless, i.e. in your cellular memory, and as such, retrievable in a way that you will feel comfortable in approaching as merely a matter of reacquaintance. The thought process necessary to recondition this access to your cellular memory need not be as stressful as your earlier approach(2). We will show you a much easier way, but first we will outline our objectives:

(a) **The power source needed** to set up the implosion process is essentially contained in the internal vortex of your cellular awareness as it interfaces with your tissue and consciousness surrounding the physical structures of your organs. The bindings of this tissue are in a sense projection, but equally, a border of an outline of mass that is filled in by imploding and exploding fields of energy, or vibration(3), maintained by your general psychic energy from "All That Is".

(b) **To release this vibration** into your visualization process is the key to unleashing the power of your thought.

(c) This unleashing process can connect, through a psychological process, to surrounding neutrons of projection with similar vibration to your directed thought patterns in a way that can be manipulated from the vortex of your neutrons to the "object's" neutrons – causing a chain reaction in physical terms capable of **moving large masses of physical weight** or propelling vehicles through space or on land.

(d) There can be some danger to the source connection – "you" in this case, so we will involve a mechanical process to act as a fuse of sorts to insure the smooth flow of energy to and from our intended circuit.

(e) It is the **circuit of thought,** propelled by either mechanical means or internal thought, that will startle your scientists in the ability of this simple procedure to alter molecular structure (visibly by your instruments) as well as move the objects of our experiment.

(f) Finally, we will introduce a "group effort" approach to this entire process which has the potential of exponentially expanding the energy we will be working with(4).

(1) COORDINATE POINTS & HEALING:

An exercise found in "Seth Speaks"[1] involves the intersection point of two imaginary lines that are mentally projected outwardly – the first from the top of your head and the second from your "third eye". Where the two lines meet indicates the nearest coordinate point in a given physical locale. I envision this point as containing unlimited energy that can be adapted for use in healing.

Once detected, I have used it by "tapping its energy" and directing it to the desired physical location in my body – visualizing a white light being propelled by this energy and then repairing the perceived damage. After a few practice trials, it seemed relatively easy to locate the coordinate point by relying on my intuition or feel. The actual relaxation required was often the most difficult aspect of the exercise. Over the past ten years I have had some remarkable successes utilizing this approach – including pulverizing an embedded kidney stone that was about to be surgically removed, restoring inner nerve damage to my right ear that had caused total deafness, etc.

1- "Seth Speaks" by Jane Roberts. Session 593, Appendix

(2) CELLULAR MEMORY:

I have had numerous experiences in accessing my cellular memory as a consequence of the death experience I encountered in 1964. A description of these events is offered in the introduction and the comments of Lesson 75.

(3) VIBRATION:

The concept of vibration becomes a key element in understanding physical reality and continuous energy. "All That Is" vibrates, and the particular vibration one entertains determines that perspective or focus of reality. There are an infinite number of ways to approach a discussion of vibration, and several will be introduced in this manuscript. In the context of explaining our physical universe, imploding and exploding fields of energy becomes a basic explanation of how we create and maintain our "illusion" – and for that matter, the whole process of creation. Whether or not a given reality will appear physical will be dependent upon whether the vibration in question is dense or slow enough for the maintenance of a physical focus.

(4) COMMENT:

I had been watching T.V. just prior to channeling this lesson when I felt a ringing in my ear and an urging to sit down at my desk and start writing. The information contained in this lesson was received as a "block" and it seemed challenging at the time to transcribe it in linear fashion since it was "there" in completed form. I immediately slipped into a dream-like state as my ego was "numbed" during this dictation. Most other lessons were completed with no apparent trance involved.

"It might seem ludicrous to you at this stage to picture yourselves moving from the simple meditation practice of holding an image — to the implementation of the power supply we speak of."

"You have a tremendous energy source at your fingertips — the source of creation itself!"

Chapter Four

RENEWABLE ENERGY

LESSON (15), NOVEMBER 15, 1987

The currently unused portions of your mind relative to the cellular memory that we speak of will make more sense to you as we proceed. The untapping of this cellular memory will inspire you on to greater heights than you currently realize, for a great emotional release will occur in your knowing, propelled into your present by several of your "past selves" with a familiarity of self as well as concept (collectively). You (Michael) have indeed merged various aspects of your probable self that is a writer in your Ottawa experience(1), and the subject of his writing is along the same lines as our experiments. In his probability, however, the scientists aren't as skeptical and are currently working on similar projects. We will help you unravel your creativity in these areas, as well as your general cellular memory. Know that you are not alone in this endeavor, and as time passes you will be made more aware of this.

(1) OTTAWA EXPERIENCE:

While at a metaphysical conference in Ottawa, Canada organized by Serge Grandbois in 1987, the "Ottawa Experience" began during an informal discussion with several of the speakers. I had been describing an incident that occurred in February of 1982 that I refer to as my "second death experience" (described in Lesson 44 - the automobile accident in 1964 being my first). In the midst of this discussion, Serge began channeling "Kris" who informed me that my description of this death like experience automatically attracts the presence of energies such as Kris.

During the following ten minutes, I was led through an initiation of sorts with a "probable self" of mine who is a writer - and in the process of accessing "his" vibration, I became awed by the multidimensional perspective I was enjoying at the time. It involved a merging not only with this probable self, but with various aspects of my greater self who were "there" to bear witness. Kris then followed with an overview of my potential relative to my understanding of energy, and what I would accomplish in the near future. I had no idea at the time that I would be writing this book, so there was some confusion. I regret that this incident wasn't taped, for it was a memorable experience.

● ● ●

LESSON (16), NOVEMBER 16, 1987

The time frame of these discoveries is no accident, as you might suspect. Your planet has nearly exhausted its natural resources in some instances, and if allowed to continue at present consumption rates, would prove quite disastrous to your future generations. A **renewable energy source** is the whole idea here and is quite available now, requiring simply a shift in thinking that we hope to provide.

Progress will be rapid in stages that have actually begun in a mass decision carried on in group activity outside of your time and space, but meant to impinge into this time for reasons just mentioned. Many individuals alive on your planet at this time have taken part in this orchestration and will intuitively feel their part in the process upon reading these passages. The desired end product is not necessarily a free gas pump in every household, but more a sense of **empowerment** in individual as well as mass terms – to not only benefit your view of yourselves, but unleash an energy source infinitely more efficient and less depletive and pollutive than your current methods.

As you have sensed many times, everything works on many levels – and the thoughts promulgated on these pages are quite multidimensional indeed and will serve many desired ends, once understood. It is our pleasure to provide whatever insights we can. Keep in mind that they are meant to be **applied**, not simply viewed as wonderful theory. Before this manuscript is complete, you will have more than enough "procedure" to move these concepts from a theoretical perspective into a quite practical and usable format. At the point of practicality, when you indeed start using these principles in a way that reveals results in your terms, you will be excited enough and bold enough to embark on ever new experiments and discover to your delight that there is literally no end to the potential of these concepts.

• • •

LESSON (17), NOVEMBER 16, 1987

The application of these principles will take several years to establish on a commercial basis, but can be started immediately on a personal and mass effort for several desired ends which we will discuss shortly. The end result will be a **self-sufficient planet** in energy consumption as well as an enlightened population with respect to the sacredness and connectedness of all life. You will, as a people, sense the energy of "All That Is" in the very essence of your thought and learn to control your thought in a much more efficient fashion. A by-product of this will be a successful utilization of universal laws for your personal sense of expanded identity as well as respect for others, nature, the animal kingdom and environment. You are leading into an **age of cooperation**, and the timing of these messages is meant to enhance that sense of direction and change.

In terms of an energy source, these principles will require a mass effort – but before the transformation of thought on a global scale, individuals can begin to practice the exercises we will give you shortly. By continued exercise and individual application of these overall concepts, your peoples will build sufficient belief and in sufficient numbers to be able to execute a shift in thought-form around the aura of your planet to denigrate the need for a more major shift of your "axis"(1) and resulting uprooting of large land masses. This shift is not predetermined, but is a possibility if

45

changes are not made in the awareness of your peoples that will lead to a more cooperative interchange of commerce.

There is complete free will as to how your peoples will choose to heal your planet, but let it be known that it **will be healed.** The violent shift in land masses and the thought of nature taking revenge is possible, but not unavoidable. You are not responsible for anyone else evolving into these awarenesses, but as individuals you are all responsible for your own well-being. The well-being of your planet will follow when enough of you take what we suggest seriously – and the benefit of integrating these concept into your emotional reality will serve you on many levels and in ways you scarcely suspect.

(1) SHIFTING OF THE EARTH'S AXIS:

I first encountered the notion of the earth having shifted it's axis in our historical past while reading a series of books written by T. Lobsang Rampa[1]. He wrote over a dozen books, offering me my first glimpse of astral travel, auras, crystals, etc. I found these works fascinating as a general introduction to metaphysics.

Other writings have subsequently asserted a shift in the earth's axis as a given in the context of upcoming earth change. It perhaps was more likely a probability when these predictions were made. This author feels that if enough individuals have the need to experience such a shift, it no doubt becomes a possibility. Everyone will meet the environment of their intent. It appears doubtful at this time, however, that this choice will be the predominate one for most.

1- "The Third Eye" by T. Lobsang Rampa. Chapter 17

• • •

LESSON (18), NOVEMBER 16, 1987

The extent and speed to which these concepts are utilized will be a matter of choice. There is no set rule, of course, as to how fast anyone must or should act on their own behalf. We simply remind you that the time is right to make an appointment with yourselves

46

to unravel your thought processes and **recognize that you are all gods** – for the sooner you do this, the sooner you will **act like gods!** This implies no value judgements of "shoulds", for all experience is a valid lesson. We merely suggest that now is the time for your planet to become more awarized on levels of the creative potential of self and the awesome power implied in the capacity to heal yourselves and your planet.

Healing(1) can take on many meanings. We imply healing on a planetary level to mean an understanding of the connectedness and sacredness of all life. Once this is understood on individual terms, it will automatically follow in group terms, for you will see all else as a reflection of your own sacredness. This feeling can spread as rapidly as any virus – and be contagious in a most beneficial way.

This is not meant to be a lecture, but a loving opportunity for growth of the most profound kind – one of self discovery. And through this discovery you will find that all of your needs get met – from energy, to food, shelter and health. There is no lack - and as your friend Beth mentioned(2), when you learn to trust in your abundance and **move into the flow** of "All That Is", everything is possible. This is true in individual terms and in terms of your planet. We are offering this perspective in general terms because it is quite important and cannot be stated any simpler. Many of your books available at this time have this or similar messages, and if read from different perspectives and different titles, perhaps you will start to believe it!

(1) HEALING:

Aside from healing in a physical orientation, the concept takes on a variety of perspectives in new age vocabulary. I perceive healing in general terms as any integration that clarifies a previous separation – such as a long standing bitterness, anxiety, fear, guilt etc.

(2) COMMENT:

Beth has acted as a catalyst not only in helping me initiate the channeling of this book (refer to the Introduction), but after the first dozen or so lessons were transcribed, I was feeling rather over-whelmed by the implications of this manuscript. I visited her at her bookstore around that time and she channeled some interesting insights that helped me to accept the entire experience. It was during this visit that Beth made the comment that . . . "once you move into the flow of your being, anything can be accomplished".

About four months after that visit, I spoke at a conference in Louisville, Ky. and found myself enjoying an altered state where I felt extremely integrated into the "flow" of my being – which lasted for several days. During that time, I seemed to be in total com-munication with my intuitive self and desired events just "hap-pened" effortlessly.

Luiz Gasparetto was there and performed a marvelous demonstration of his channeled art. A tape of "Deep Breakfast" by Ray Lynch was played very loudly as Luiz slipped into a wild trance where he would paint with his eyes closed, his toes, looking at the ceiling, flaying his head in circles, and moving his hands with blinding speed. Gerry Bowman[1] and Joe Albiani (his partner) were standing next to me, Serge Grandbois was a few feet away, and Marcel Vogel (well-known author, inventor, and crystal expert) was across the room gazing into one of his crystals. Together with the hundred or so other people in the room, there was an electrify-ing atmosphere that was filled with unseen spirits.

One of the paintings created by Luiz that afternoon was a magnificent and compassionate portrayal of Christ that was made available for sale. Almost everyone that room wanted that painting and consequently names were written on small pieces of paper and placed under each picture for a drawing. I intuitively knew that my name would be drawn, and when it was called it felt like I had just won the lottery. Luiz channeled Chagall, Matisse, Rembrandt, and De Vinci among others. The Christ is a "De Vinci" and has a healing quality to it that seems to address the viewer in a manner that challenges them emotionally.

1- Gerry Bowman and Joe Albiani are friends of mine who have travelled to many of the same conferences I've been to. Together, they organized a trip to Egypt in May of 1988. Gerry is a powerful deep trance channel and was, in my opinion, at his very best when he channeled an initiation in the great pyramid at Giza. This was a most transforming experience for many of us in attendance. Barbara Marciniak began speaking for the Pleiadians a few days later. Shallom Berkman started channeling Quadra – a female Pleiadian energy and our mutual friend Jeff McDowell began telepathic communication with his guides as well as various extraterrestrials. I began channeling Orion energies and aspects of my greater self, all within a few months of that initiation.

"What we are suggesting is that once accepted and understood, our model will gradually replace your dependence on fossil fuels."

"Continuous Energy represents a collective challenge."

Chapter Five

DIRECTED THOUGHT

LESSON (19), NOVEMBER 17, 1987

As a rule, the importance of directing one's thought is not understood on your planet. Random thought, or scattered thought, keeps your energies in a state of flux – and the aura of your earth reflects this perfectly. As indicated earlier, the essence of your thought is the essence of "All That Is", quite literally. If this principle were understood on a basic emotional and intellectual level, your sense of "empowerment" would be accomplished immediately! **Directed thought,** therefore, is the key to the exercises we will outline for purposes of manifestation on personal levels and energy promulgation on a global scale. Transport will be considered as a separate concept, although the underlying procedure is the same.

Because your beliefs tell you that thought is "nonphysical", it is considered "nonreal" – and once expressed or forgotten, dissipated into nothingness. This is quite contrary to the nature of thought and we hope to clear up this misconception. Directed thought becomes a powerhouse of quite amazing magnitude. And if done in conjunction with like-minded individuals of similar intent, you have the potential to compound the effect many times over. When your intent is organized or expressed as a unified thought pattern, it aligns the "creative forces" in a way that gathers momentum from outside of your time and space. It then impinges into your reality in a pre-matter state that solidifies in your terms as your intent is maintained or strengthened.

The process we wish to outline for you will involve **exercises** of concentration and certain visualization patterns(1) – with the ability to direct these patterns into designated objectives. Implosion of neutrons will occur when you have reached certain intensities in your concentration abilities and the subsequent ability to emit your thought pattern, keeping intact the vortex or gestalt of that which you will manifest. Implosion occurs when sufficient peak intensities are reached and a circuit is formed by your ability to direct this vibration in a precise and undeviating manner. This will take practice and a knowing that you indeed have the capacity to accomplish these ends.

There are many of you in physical focus at this time that have utilized these skills in other times and will sense a certain familiarity in the reading of these passages. Your cellular memory will be activated which will greatly facilitate the implementation of your early successes. We, of course, will assist you – and at times unbeknownst to you. As your sensitivity builds up, you will recognize our input(2). You will notice an acceleration in upcoming lessons and we are most anxious to proceed.

(1) COMMENT:

The "Concentration" and "Mobility of Consciousness" exercises that follow become the preliminary steps necessary for the successful demonstration of continuous energy as well as manifestation. The remaining exercises found in this volume will all be integrated into the abilities of these first procedures.

(2) ANGELS & MANIFESTED BEINGS:

Since transcribing this lesson, there have been several encounters with extraterrestrials, as well as manifested beings in the guise of humans. The first such being was sitting in my assigned seat on the airplane ride mentioned in the introduction. In that instance, "her" energy guided me into the out-of-body experience that acted as my formal introduction to the Orion energies.

The second being was encountered in March of 1989 in Germany while I was lost in the pursuit of a former concentration camp site. I was searching for Bergen-Belson and was misdirected to Bergen-Dumme, near the East German border. The town was deserted as I approached, except for a man that appeared to be in his fifties getting out of his Mercedes. He was wearing a beret, army jacket and jeans that didn't go with his age or automobile. He spoke perfect English with no accent and without being asked, responded . . . "oh, you want the concentration camp, that's quite far, about 70 kilometers to the west".

I was amused at the provincial attitude of this man who thought 70 kilometers was "so far away". It then hit me that there was something very strange about him. Besides his lack of accent, I had not given him enough information for the response he gave me. He also had a nonphysical quality about him similar to the woman on the airplane who sat in my assigned seat. It was as though he was physical, yet I could somehow "see" right through him. I came to the realization that this was an "angel" who would remind me of my divinity before I would witness the rememberings of Bergen-Belson.

The third encounter was a few months later in October of 1989 while I was walking in downtown Milwaukee carrying a sack of very heavy books. There was a black man in his early thirties sitting in the passenger seat of a rusted out 1964 Cadillac. As I passed, he asked me for $19 to which I smiled and kept walking. Just a few feet further, he just "appeared" next to me without getting out of the car! I was somewhat stunned as he asked me if I could "help" him.

He was very nonspecific and kept asking if I would help him out. I asked him how much money he needed and he replied, "I didn't say anything about money" (even though he'd asked for $19 while in the car?). He said he was "just passing through" and needed some help. When I asked where he was from, he replied. . . "St. Louis". I couldn't help notice loose straw in his hair and a most gentle demeanor – exactly like the man in Bergen-Dumme, Germany. There was something ethereal about him, like he was there and wasn't there at the same time. I told him I would withdraw some cash from a "Tyme" machine and give him five dollars. Asking if he would wait right there until I made my delivery, he agreed. When I returned, he was gone. I somehow "knew" that he recognized I had no money on me, and was just testing to see if I would help him.

About two weeks after that encounter, I was awakened by a telephone call at 1:30 in the morning. It was the police informing me that my car had been demolished by a drunk driver and that I better come outside and remove any belongings before it would be towed away. The next day I went to the junk yard to take any leftover items, and was informed that the car that hit mine was right next to my car. It was the same rusted out 1964 Cadillac that my friend from St. Louis had materialized out of! As it turned out, I had just taken out collision insurance on that car before I left for Germany, and my financial settlement was quite satisfactory. I still haven't figured out why that angel would have projected himself in a similar car that would demolish mine a few weeks later, other than the humor of it all.

● ● ●

LESSON (20), NOVEMBER 18, 1987

Your conversations with your friend Mark(1) have been touching on precisely the direction we are leading you in an understanding of what we will accomplish. Your interpretation of the illusion of physical reality as seen through your many and varied experiences(2) puts you in a unique position to understand and implement our experiments that we will soon introduce. As you know, the physical world is an illusion to the perspective of an energy personality outside of your vibration, yet quite real to you as sensed by your physical senses and your ego.

The whole point here is that the "gap" between this **illusion of projection** and the belief in the projection can be narrowed considerably. And in this narrowing, there lies tremendous potential in the area of manipulating your physical environment in ways currently thought impossible. We are saying that not only is it possible, but that many of you have worked with this awareness in other times and have been quite masterful at this type of manipulation. It is with delight that we re-introduce these "lost sciences" to you.

The next several lessons will deal with how to approach the physical and molecular structures of your world – with the insight of the projection that is creating the structure in the first place. In learning how to **manipulate your subconscious projections,** you will learn how to change them and re-arrange them and utilize the subsequent energy release for many of your physical needs. The physical laws that will attempt to explain these manipulations are valid only up to a point. What we are approaching is beyond your physical laws and done in a way that will affect your molecular structures in a most interesting manner. There are many potential applications to these principles. We will touch on those that have the most potential impact on the "healing" perspectives of your planet.

(1) COMMENT:

Mark M. Giese, who prefers to be referred to as "Mark M", is a good friend of mine who lives about twenty-five miles outside of Milwaukee. We initially met at a local Seth group that would meet monthly, but that has since disbanded. He has graciously acted as my sounding board for whatever psychic experience or concept I wish to discuss. In the context of these discussions, some of which have been quite lengthy, I have come to understand various experiences and ideas in a much clearer perspective. Mark has delved into the Seth material as much as I and has an amazing recall of obscure comment that can be found in any of the twenty-one Jane Roberts/Seth books. So he is an invaluable resource person as well as an excellent sounding board and friend.

(2) ILLUSION:

After experiencing most of the levels of consciousness described in "Seth Speaks", I became awed by my growing comprehension of the illusionary aspects of our physical world. I simply couldn't accept my visual focus with the same belief and assumptions that I previously entertained. There were numerous occasions where I was able to see "through" objects, blend with them and experience their perspective. Sometimes my entire physical field would appear dream-like, composed of waves of light and energy. There were other realities where physical props seemed more solid and hence more "real" than ours.

An interesting experience dealing with "illusion" began in April of 1982 as I was driving home from Chicago around 2:00 A.M. It was foggy and drizzly as I traveled north on highway 41 when I approached a large gold pyramid with an eerie glow around it. I was unaware of this structure at the time, which has since become a tourist attraction. As I drove closer to the proximity of this pyramid, I felt a disconcerting uneasiness – and spontaneously slipped into an altered state.

Nearing a turn in the road, to my surprise, I observed several emergency vehicles to the side of the highway overlooking a ditch. As I passed this scene, I noticed an overturned car at the bottom of the hill. Simultaneous to this observation, I immediately found myself in telepathic communication with a man in that car who was disoriented and seemingly couldn't decide whether or not to die. He was rather panicky and wanted my input. I was rather shaken at this juncture and continued to drive, not recalling any more of the "conversation".

The next afternoon, I found myself becoming drowsy and laid down on my living room floor to take a catnap. Upon closing my eyes, I immediately slipped into a very "fine" pulsation as my total perspective began to vibrate. I opened my eyes with a start and to my surprise noticed that my entire visual view was beginning to disappear! Holding on to this perspective for a few minutes, to my utter amazement, objects in front of me began to disappear entirely. When my body started this vanishing act, I began to panic since nothing seemed to be taking its place. I chose not to deal with the experience and simply closed my eyes, still feeling the vibration, and fell asleep.

● ● ●

LESSON (21), NOVEMBER 19, 1987

Relay stations in electrical terms transmit energy through wires electrically charged and then switched to alternate tracks through the discretion of the operator or mechanical device in control. In mental terms, your consciousness will be directing your electrical impulses to and around designated points. We will approach your physical brain as a generator of sorts, capable of emitting impulses through your thoughts to desired destinations, using **relay stations** as stopping or transfer points where the impulses of others can take over (or) where you can transfer to another frequency. The method of transmission will be determined by your intent, and the force of your transmission will be adjusted by the visualization required for each task.

We will start with relatively easy tasks, to give you a feel for the methodology implicit in these exercises – and expand into rather esoteric dimensions of the thus far unused portions of the mind. We will be setting up **circuits** within and beyond your physical awareness, impinging into areas of "middle ground", so to speak, where pre-matter structures are awaiting manifestation into physical realms through empowerment of intent. Various schematics will be helpful after awhile to help you visualize the process we will be utilizing. We suggest you break for awhile and return after digesting the concepts introduced thus far.

● ● ●

LESSON (22), NOVEMBER, 20 1987

The concepts covered thus far deal with an overview of that which we will accomplish. Your part in this (Michael) is to translate these concepts into terms that the public can relate to and implement for the betterment of your world. This is **a pioneering effort,** and as such, will involve trial and error. It is important not to get discouraged at early difficulties or perceived failure. As you know, you must start where you are and move on from there. This is true in any sense of accomplishment.

Know that you (Michael) have experienced many of the altered states that you will re-experience over the next several months. Now, however, you will sense our accompaniment, whereas in the past you felt you were embarking on these journeys alone(1). We have watched you and joined you far more often than you recognize. You (collectively) are never alone, whether you care to acknowledge that or not. Because our intent interconnects with yours on many levels, we see fit to monitor your experiences and at times even help orchestrate them. Your telephone experiences with your friend Beth on 11-2-87 are a case in point(2).

Your interpretation of the awesome energy you encountered and expressed in your introduction was indeed the very energy you will learn to become comfortable with and direct. It is not so much that this energy is just outside the gates of your space and time, as you felt at the time of your experience – as it is lying within the space of the very room in which you now find yourself. It is a matter of recognizing that which has always been available.

Because of a turn in your planet's evolutionary path, you have chosen as a people to re-awaken this knowing and utilize this energy to create a more **loving and cooperative experiment.** As your people realize that they are infinitely more powerful than they have allowed, a major shift will occur in the commerce of your world to one of far greater cooperation and support for the rights of others. You will no longer have the need to fight for your piece of the pie, recognizing that there is more than enough for everyone. Not everyone will come to these realizations at the same time, however, so there will continue to be power struggles and wars. Ever increasing numbers will get in touch with their sources and soul energy, though, and spread their awareness as you (Michael) are now doing. Hopefully, this process will affect your planet in such a way as to eliminate the need for more violent shifts.

(1) COMMENT:

Since discovering the Seth material in 1976, I've quite consciously set out on a journey that would "prove" to myself the validity of the concepts I was entertaining. My intent was driven by several "warrior" roles (reincarnationally) that got carried away in terms of human suffering. This momentum propelled me into the obsession for "truth" that I am experiencing in this lifetime. During the peak years of this seeking, I encountered such a vast assortment of altered states that it temporarily jaded my appreciation and acceptance of my physical focus. And during the midst of this activity, I'd always felt that I was embarking on these journeys alone, even taking pride in my "independence".

Years later I began to realize that I had company. In 1985, I was told by Ralph Knoll[1] as he was channeling "Rama", that he had helped orchestrate several of my most dynamic experiences. Since then, I've come to recognize that I have many friends in spirit.

1- Ralph Knoll is one of the most interesting persons I've ever met. He provided the first "live" channeling I'd experienced. I later discovered that he naturally sees auras, does aura readings and is an expert dowser. He was once a master chef, one of the strongest men on earth, a professional wrestler and a biker – all complimenting his varied psychic abilities.

(2) OUT-OF-BODY EXPERIENCES:

This buzz word typically denotes an altered state where the individual's consciousness leaves the body and explores other physical locations (or) alternate realities outside of our camouflage parameters. There is much folklore attached to this experience, including physical observation of the astral or silver cord, the actual "travel" to other locations, etc.

Basically, one doesn't "go" anywhere – since space is an illusion as much as time. The individual merely divests himself of his particular camouflage, alters his vibration, and entertains an alternate focus. In this context, the person is bringing the other reality "to" him, rather than going anywhere.

Since our understanding of space is quite distorted, it becomes quite possible to be in two locations at once and bilocate for a variety of purposes. In the telephone out-of-body experience mentioned, I simply found myself talking on the telephone and focusing on an alternate reality at the same time. I am interpreting this alternate focus as an out-of-body perspective for the sake of simplicity. This experience has consciously occurred at least a half dozen times, but this one was the most momentous to date.

In like-manner, I see it as impossible to channel an "outside" entity or personality since whatever degree of consciousness we are entertaining, it is always a reflection of "self". There is literally nothing outside of ourselves but projection, which we have accepted as physical reality. In this context, we literally are "All That Is".

● ● ●

LESSON (23), NOVEMBER 22, 1987

You are embarking on an experiment in your terms that will open the gates to further experimentation by others. Collectively, you are reawakening and narrowing the gap of who you are – and that which you previously believed you were capable of. You are all sacred beings, with little difference between your sense of sacredness and that which you worship in your churches. You will sense your "oneness" with this source in such a way that will leave little doubt that you are indeed Gods – capitalized!

The powers inherent in your consciousness have thus far been somewhat latent by choice because of your belief in your separateness(1), but the time has come to bring together that which you have considered separate. This time has come not so much because we have sensed its arrival, but because you as a people have chosen in a collective decision making process to make these happenings occur at this time – perhaps just in time, to save your planet from more violent changes or shifts than might occur if you had waited any longer.

You will all act when it feels right for each of you – and by acting, we imply a beginning of the process you would consider **emotional introspection(2)** and start to expand your perspective of who you are. This process of exploring your emotional make-up will extend to what you would consider psychic growth and expansion, often in surprising manner. As more of you awaken to your own potential, more and more of you will be encouraged to try and soon the momentum will have begun. It can be a grand game, and we will joyfully play along with you if you will allow us(3).

(1) SEPARATION & DUALITIES:

The beliefs we have entertained for seeming endless reincarnational cycles tells us that reality lies "outside" of ourselves. This has evolved into a framework of currently experiencing our physical senses as the totality of our world view. The essence of earth change can be looked at as an understanding that we are not separate from "All That Is" in any context. We are "one" with each other, the planet and all aspects of our greater selves.

According to a composite of various channeled sources, our civilizations' belief in "separateness" began approximately 25,000 years ago during the last days of Atlantis. Our present time period can be compared to Atlantis in its critical period. However, it appears that the momentum we have chosen will carry us into a period of integration rather than the ultimate destruction as ascribed to in the Atlantian legend.

(2) EMOTIONAL INTROSPECTION:

Emotional introspection becomes the only way to know ourselves and subsequently sense our oneness with "All That Is". Beginning with our thoughts and the emotions they engender, there is an endless web of connectedness to witness that provides the "proof" that we are indeed "ONE". A sorting out process is initially required – one that is described beautifully in "The Nature of Personal Reality", a Seth book by Jane Roberts.

Not only is our connectedness observed in this manner, but the relationship between our thoughts and subsequent experience becomes obvious. This in turn becomes a tremendous tool for personal empowerment – recognizing that we indeed have the capacity to take control of our overall life experience.

(3) SUPPORT FOR OUR PERSONAL GROWTH:

Support from various aspects of "self" becomes obvious when we reach a certain momentum of sincerity relative to personal growth. As we expand our "awareness", we automatically expand our concept of what we consider "reality", since our world view grows accordingly. Expansion in these terms brings us the recognition that support is automatically available because it is indeed a larger picture of us that contains all reality and hence all the support we can use. It then becomes a matter of allowing the support we desire to filter through in recognizable form.

The awareness of some of my closest nonphysical support began in the spring of 1986. I attended a workshop given by Meredith Young (author of "Agartha – a Journey To The Stars") and met two individuals that would have a profound impact on my life. Robert Dubiel and Kathleen Schoenstadt (Katar) have both been channeling for over 15 years. At a restaurant after the workshop had ended, Kathleen slipped into a trance and began channeling "Clark" – a nonphysical energy who in his last incarnation on earth lived in Denmark where we had known each other. Since that introduction, I've had numerous conversations with Clark and consider him a best friend.

Chapter Six

CIRCUITS OF INTENT

LESSON (24), NOVEMBER 22, 1987

The nuts and bolts of the experiments that you have so eagerly awaited will be given to you shortly. At this time we remind you again that to get discouraged or anxious at early experimentation is a normal process. Persistence and a little help from us will bring the results you are anxious about achieving – and these results will lead to the confidence to experiment further. What will be considered the first order of business will be an **exercise in concentration**(1) – keeping a specific thought pattern in your mind for greater and greater periods of time until you reach a point where you can hold a pattern for fifteen minutes or so. This ability is necessary for the next step, as each step will build on the previous one.

To begin then, we suggest you select a simple piece of fruit, such as an apple, and hold it in your mind's eye for periods leading up to fifteen minutes. Concentrate and pay very close attention to every aspect of this apple – from its color to its shades and shadows, its texture, size, shape and placement in the perspective of your created scene. It will be helpful to set up a physical apple first, and look at it for a few minutes and then close your eyes and continue with the experiment. As simple as this sounds, it will greatly induce the ability to further visualize the process we will uncover next.

(1) CONCENTRATION EXERCISE:

This becomes the first exercise in a series of mental maneuvers leading up to an understanding of continuous energy (refer to the index for a complete list of exercises). The following is an account of how I approached the concentration exercise. Some of the techniques I developed will hopefully aid you in your practice. I purchased a timer and a new apple every few days for variety and experimented daily for three weeks:

11-23-87: I sensed my ability to **solidify** the apple in my mind. It seemed theoretically possible to manifest the apple out of the clear blue.

11-24-87: I felt that I could **intensify** my image with an infusion of "thought/energy".

11-25-87: There occurred a spontaneous appearance of **a yellow screen** with the apple in front of it. The screen seemed to illuminate the apple in a colorful way, very bright, similar to a computer screen.

11-28-87: **Lightening up on my trance** state greatly enhanced my ability to hold the image. **Envisioning a slight aura** around the apple also helped stabilize the image. A slight white aura was all that was needed.

11-29-87: Visualizing several **spotlights** directed toward my image of the apple had a very powerful influence on my ability to hold the pattern. This proved to be the most helpful technique for me.

12-03-87: Becoming the apple at times became easier than holding the image, because of my tendency to slip into an altered state. Today, **I became the apple** and sensed "my" texture, juices and mass – which from my perspective became infinite. I quite happily entertained the thought of being eaten and somehow merging in the process of tasting my own manifestation and creation. Spatially, I was a universe of "joyful fruition and applehood".

12-08-87: **Establishing an anchor point** within the object enabled me to concentrate for greater lengths of time. After about ten days, I was able to hold a relatively firm focus on my apple for close to fifteen minutes. Lack of daily practice and follow-through, however, lessened my abilities and seemed to set me back several days. It also became much easier to concentrate on faces or objects with letters or numbers on them, i.e. a postage stamp or a picture with unusual features.

12-10-87: When I start to lose my image, I'm finding that I can **imagine myself opening up my eyes** and looking at the object again. In this way, I found that I was able to refocus rather intensely for a brief moment with amazing clarity and actually observe various details that escaped me earlier.

12-13-87: I'm able to fixate on my object now for longer periods if I establish a holding pattern **without thinking of any particular technique.**

01-03-88: I am realizing that my image can be held visually between and within other thoughts, i.e. similar to daydreaming or **thought within thought.** I am also visualizing a **windshield wiper** to erase intruding thoughts. This also keeps me aware of my image slipping. I have been relying more and more on keeping my **inner eyes open** to maintain my hold.

● ● ●

LESSON (25), NOVEMBER 23, 1987

The concentration ability you are developing will greatly facilitate the later ability to direct these images into the angles and ends of your desired next step. What we are accomplishing is the **implementation of a circuit** as discussed earlier. This circuit, however, will not necessarily follow the path of a typical electrical circuit you are familiar with. It will involve **feeling-tones(1),** as well as directing and folding energy and "space/time" that won't be amenable to diagram form. We will give you symbols for these **energy folds** that you will develop an emotional relationship and feel for. With continued practice you will be quite able to visualize these folds as destination points. These points will further enable you to reach greater and greater intensities, interpreting them as **relay stations,** where you will be able to gather your perspective and continue on with the process.

The end result will be the instantaneous and spontaneous materialization of a pre-matter outline of that which you are materializing, as well as a release of energy that we will later tell you how to recognize as such and direct in a desired manner. This energy release will have more practical potential in your terms, but we must build up to that point and first develop an understanding and feel for the initial process just described. We are viewing this entire procedure as a concentration and visualization process, but as you can see, it is infinitely more vital and multidimensional than you are accustomed to observing in a visualization exercise.

This exercise will also, as you might suspect, lend itself to numerous altered states of a most pleasant nature, but keep in mind that at other times you can experiment toward those ends. For the time being, keep reminding yourself that the intent and objective here is to develop your ability to concentrate for longer and longer periods.

(1) FEELING-TONES:

Feeling-tones are your most intimate perception of self that shape your emotional attitudes toward life. Differing from generally conscious feelings that come and go, these lie beneath your easily recognized emotions and color your overall life experience. It's not that these tones are static, but more that their rhythms would be in longer cycles. They are uniquely you and represent the most inner core of your emotional body. Similar to your overall emotional make-up, they can be relatively expansive and open as opposed to being blocked. In terms of utilizing them within the circuits being developed, **your challenge** becomes one of recognizing them and developing a rapport with this aspect of yourself.

The power of these tones can clarify the connectedness between us and our environment. It is easy to assume that our body ends with the outline of our flesh. Our feelings, however, have electromagnetic properties that leave us and interact with our environment on a continual basis. Quite literally, all of our emotions free hormones that not only effect our physical body, but effect the emotional climate of the space around us. Consider what happens if we hold our breath too long. In the same way, portions of our bodily make-up continuously mix with the air that engulfs us.

Examine for a moment the biological construction of our bodies. Broken down into the underlying atomic structure, there is a constant spinning, vibrating, and orbiting between the atoms and molecules. Our bodies that seem so solid are literally composed of an endless stream of activity. And this activity is not confined within the limits of our flesh. Great interchanges of energy go on endlessly with the "outside" of us that is also made of the same elements, vibrating at a different resonance. Our bodies could not be maintained without this sharing.

As all fragments of the earth consciousness possess their own frame of reference, they also enjoy the gestalt knowing of their connectedness to the whole. This means that we are part of this whole, and intimately connected to our environment. Only because we have kept these knowings at subconscious levels for so long, do we resist the potential of unlocking this oneness. Once we become comfortable with our own inner tones, we will appreciate this awesome potential that will open the gates to the effectiveness of continuous energy.

The personality of these tones can be identified – and, they will lend themselves to being "objectified" as a pattern that can called upon at will. They will then help facilitate our circuits, for they are in intimate contact with our environment, and as much a part of our "projection" as the air we breath. The process of developing a "feel" for these feeling-tones will be a gradual one as we entertain the various exercises in this manuscript[1].

1- An overall discussion of feeling tones can be found in "The Nature of Personal Reality", A Seth book by Jane Roberts, Chapter 1, Session 613. A specific technique for sensing your own personal tones can be found in Chapter 2, Session 614 of that same book.

• • •

LESSON (26), NOVEMBER 24, 1987

The development of these **circuits of intent** will lend itself to a wide variety of applications on your physical plane – from a procedure of manifestation to an energy source of quite unlimited means. The duration and intensity of these circuits can vary widely for your purpose at hand, as well as an unlimited variety of circumstances that will instigate the implementation of yet another circuit. The combination of mental process and mechanical aids will provide you with additional combinations of factors to add further potentials for these procedures. Group activities will greatly enhance the effect, of course, whether done mentally or in combination with mechanical devices.

The thrust of the process is always mental, because yours is a mental universe and not a mechanical one. The accompanying mechanical devices that we will discuss (at a later time) do have their place, since your mental universe does, after all, take on a physical appearance. So you have a blending of physical appearance and mental process in your world at large, and a combination for our model as well. For your larger projects you will have more extravagant contraptions, but at no time will the process require elaborate gear such as your computer circuitry.

We will utilize **conducting rods** of sorts, similar to your man Tesla(1), but in somewhat a different manner. These rods will act as simulators of thought, to hold a particular vibration between points in our circuit that can be held in abeyance indefinitely, or activated by intent to complete the circuit. Individuals stationed at different points along the way could theoretically do the same thing, but it will be more practical in large projects to implement mechanical rods for obvious reasons.

(1) NIKOLA TESLA: (1-17-90)

This was the first mention of Nikola Tesla in the manuscript. At the time the above lesson was dictated (November of 1987), I had heard of him, but knew virtually nothing of his vast accomplishments. In December of 1989, I read "Prodigal Genius, The Life of Nikola Tesla" by John J. O'neill. O'neill was the Pulitzer prize-winning science editor and writer for the New York Herald Tribune. He and Tesla were friends for many years and Prodigal Genius was created almost immediately after Tesla's death in 1943. It was amazing to me after reading his biography that the awesome contributions Tesla made in many fields of science could have been forgotten so shortly after his death.

The day I finished Tesla's biography, I did a routine channeling into a tape recorder. The Orion energies casually announced that they wanted to introduce me to an energy that wished a voice. To my utter surprise, in a strange rather sing-song voice came the words of none other than NIKOLA TESLA! He announced that he has no interest in reincarnating back to the earth plane, but is, among other things, working with the electromagnetic grid pattern of the earth itself in a process of readying the planet for the vibrational shifts alluded to in this manuscript.

An overview of Tesla's accomplishments, as well as several transcripts of these "conversations" can be found in the Appendices.

• • •

LESSON (27), NOVEMBER 24, 1987

Your question as to what the original source of power is behind these circuits requires some background information to answer in a way that you will understand and accept. There need be **no central power source** as you are accustomed to, but instead numerous and periodic relay stations that feed each other in a rather symbiotic manner. Each of these stations in turn are powered by a process of mental and mechanical means, but in a way that requires some unstructuring of your beliefs in terms of mental "effort".

General intent, reinforced by periodic "charges" of energy, lead to the concepts we will develop. A mechanical device can be utilized to store intent in a way not understood. We are leading to an understanding of group energy directed into the atmosphere in a way that can be then tapped by the conducting rods we have spoken of.

The energy is already in your atmosphere, but in such a state of flux because the general lack of direction in the majority of your people with regard to their awareness of thought patterns. In other words, the aura around your earth reflects a jumble of thought as electromagnetic storms on the surface of your sun would show up on some of your instruments. If enough individuals project a pattern of intent in a cohesive manner that we will describe, this then can be tapped by your conducting rods (or) individually by simply attuning to that vibration. We do not mean to imply that this energy field is not in existence now, only that to be made commercially usable, it would require some re-adjustment of group intent and directed thought along these lines.

Tesla experimented with these concepts in a round about way and did indeed develop a conducting rod that enabled him to "energize" his immediate surroundings, with little additional energy sources. What we are suggesting is a much amplified circuitry empowered by more refined conducting rods picking up signals from continuous **bands of intent** surrounding a given geographical area. The source of power to generate each station along the way involves a mental exercise that is projected and stored in the conducting rods and then transmitted to the next station by simple mechanical devices. The mechanics of this system will be explained after we further explain these introductory concepts, which seem to be rather vague to you at this point. But since you asked, we give you an outline for consideration.

● ● ●

70

LESSON (28), NOVEMBER 25, 1987

The concept of a "circuit of intent" being tapped by individuals or mechanical means has some similarities to the process of your physical senses. Your inner self emits energy on a subconscious level to continually create and form the physical objects that you "then" perceive as real, but they are real only through the guise of your physical senses – with your **belief** being the cement that really holds your system together(1). Our model is quite similar, except that this process becomes conscious, and in reverse at times. Instead of shooting out energy to then be picked up by your physical or outer senses, you will be shooting out energy to be picked up by your intuitive or inner senses – and manipulated by mental and mechanical means to be either stored or sent on to the next relay station where the process is then repeated.

We are indeed working with the "gap" between your belief in physical reality and the illusionary aspects of your reality. **Understanding the illusion** will help your readers appreciate these concepts in infinitely greater terms – and is almost a prerequisite in implementing this model in practical terms(2). A bit of practice will also be required in concentration abilities, and a familiarization with the internal patterns of your mind that are capable of a considerable degree of molding in a compatible way for the purposes of receiving and directing the energy we speak of. Some degree of understanding and familiarization are needed to make these concepts workable, so we suggest you absorb an overview of these lessons before you judge the applicability of these concepts.

(1) QUESTION:

Would it be more accurate to state that it's our "intent" to experience physical reality rather than our "belief" that holds our system together?

Yes, but belief in this case accurately describes your intent to focus in a physical manner. If you didn't collectively "believe" in the validity of physical reality, you would not enjoy the same levels of value fulfillment that you currently entertain.

(2) COMMENT:

The illusionary aspects of our physical reality will be referenced continuously throughout this manuscript. Rereading the notes of Lesson 2 dealing with "projection" may be helpful in this context.

Chapter Seven

THE NEUTRON

LESSON (29), NOVEMBER 26, 1987

The motion of atoms in terms of your understanding needs some clarification. As you know, the electrons spin around the nucleus which in turn are composed of protons and neutrons. We have spoken of neutron implosion, and we must now give you some prerequisite concepts on the **nature of neutrons.** Subatomic particles as a whole are not subatomic to the perspective of the given particle in question – and from the perspective of your visualization abilities, you have the capacity to manipulate the movement and thrust of these particles by your intent and objective. These particles will joyfully cooperate with your intent once you learn how to communicate with these aspects – and jointly you can then work together toward ends you will "agree" upon.

It is not that the neutron is a personality gestalt as such, but more an **awarized energy**(1) that knows its status and capabilities – and yet is not concerned with its ego at any given time since it has no ego. Therefore, it is infinitely more aware of its "placement" which can literally be in more than one place at a time. This ability of your neutron is similar to the underlying **units of consciousness**(2) since the units of consciousness are their building blocks. Because the neutrons can be in more than one place at a time, they have the innate capacity to explode, implode, transport, skip into alternate realities, and generally cooperate in gymnastics of cosmic proportions – at "your" discretion! It becomes your challenge then, **to learn to communicate with these neutrons,** which will be an exercise that we will introduce as your next project.

(1) AWARIZED ENERGY:

The physical universe, seen as a projection, recognizes that projection as being conscious. **"All That Is"** is **conscious**, regardless of focus. Even physical objects are energized and aware. There is no "dead matter", and all consciousness is aware to the extent of its chosen value fulfillment. Since "energy" is the medium of all expression and all expression is conscious, all energy is awarized. A discussion of the value fulfillment of inanimate objects can be found in the notes of Lesson 61.

(2) UNITS OF CONSCIOUSNESS:

The basic building blocks of the universe can be looked at as "units of consciousness". A unit here would not be considered a "particle", but a universe of spirit that knows itself, yet needs no physical parameters to express itself. Physical expression is but one mode of expression – and because these units are inviolate, they have no "time" orientation and literally express themselves in many focuses at once. They move faster than the speed of light and are infinitely beyond the range of matter. Precisely because of these attributes, physical probing into their existence would be useless. With this in mind, the billions of dollars spent on particle accelerators in an attempt to understand our physical reality becomes very limiting without a parallel input of CONSCIOUSNESS integrated into that search!

• • •

LESSON (30), NOVEMBER 27, 1987

The velocity of atomic structures as seen by your instruments is a relative concept, no different than two speeding automobiles side by side on a freeway. The idea here is to **step into the time frame of the atom** and slow down the movement of the electron from your perspective, so as to allow your penetration into their movement Once achieved, it will not appear as though the movement is at blinding speed because you will have altered your spatial perspective to accommodate this space/time framework. It will take practice after accepting the potential of these maneuvers, but the first step is intellectually accepting the possibility – and then becoming emotionally comfortable with the process which we will introduce gradually. The leap between these manipulations and your beliefs is what we are dealing with. For if you had been taught as a child to perform these maneuvers, you would think nothing of them.

Since these ideas are radical to your present beliefs about the abilities of the mind, you are feeling rather questioning. You may be comforted though in the knowing that you have had this knowledge stored in your cellular memory all along. The entry and exit procedures of these exercises will be the aspect of the experience that will require some reorientation and understanding. You will become familiar with space/time coordinates and gestalt formations, i.e. as to how one fits into the other. It is not that these atomic particles are so small, as much as they fit "within the thought – within the thought". You will learn to slow down your vibration for the entry process and speed up for the exit, perhaps opposite to what logically would seem to make sense to you.

The vibration of most realities "outside" of your space/time are indeed faster, but from the entry point of merging with your atom you will momentarily be slowing down your vibration **and** the atom's vibration simultaneously – since you really are sensing your oneness at this moment. If you didn't slow down your vibration you wouldn't be able to perceive your entry point. This becomes like skipping rope with several ropes in the game, and if you miss and hit the rope, you simply start over. This game will be no different and there is no danger(1) involved.

QUESTION:

Are we dealing with actual atoms, or a process of visualizing atoms?

The distinction between an "actual atom" and a visualization process needs explanation. The physical attributes of your atoms are a form of projection, and as such, are amenable to visualization since we are still dealing with thought. You will not be dealing with atoms of any given structure as such, but with a concept that incorporates your atomic structure in a legitimate manner that your visualization process mimics. The end result is the same, and you don't have to worry about the distinction at the time.

(1) CONCERN FOR SAFETY IN THE PROCESS: (7-1-90)

Remembering a comment made in Lesson 14, point (d) of the objectives summary, I became curious as to what danger is involved?

The seeming contradiction here can be clarified in the recognition that this is an introductory manuscript. At the time that your mechanical devices will be introduced[1], you will have attained the expertise and awareness bringing you to the point of potential concern. At this juncture, however, you can feel completely at ease in pursuing these concepts to the limits of your understanding. There is no danger at these beginning stages, which will lead to some surprising results prior to the actual commercial success of continuous energy.

1- Question: And when will these devices be introduced?

The time frame of these devices will depend somewhat on the probabilities of when they will be required. We will include them in your next manuscript, if the timing is appropriate.

● ● ●

LESSON (31), NOVEMBER 28, 1987

The motion of atomic particles as seen through your instruments is in a way projection since your entire physical field is a projection. However, the intent of the projection as it meets your time and space is a valid perspective for all participants – and some visitors such as ourselves who have a keen interest in your planet's evolution. This interest goes beyond what you consider a friendly gesture, for in most basic terms we are part and parcel of your being, individually and collectively. We share the same "source" and have the same overall perspective on many matters. In some areas however, our overview is wider and grander since we are part of the energies that are behind your intent to formulate your physical world in the first place(1). This creation is going on "now" as there literally is no beginning or end. Within this knowing you have a tremendous energy source at your fingertips – **the source of creation itself!**

There is no real separation between your reality and ours, except your ego acting as interpreter – and there is no difference between the creator and the creations, since the continuous creation contains and implies "All That Is" in essence and potential in each and every creation. Perhaps the main difference between our perspective and yours is that we are intimately aware of this process and this is what we are imparting to you.

Understanding your power from the perspective of this creative process leaves no room for doubt or questioning. You become ONE with the creator and break all barriers of limitation, for the ONE you are merging with is simply a **larger picture of yourself.** That larger picture approaches the identity behind these lessons, for we are larger portions of yourself (Michael) and all those who share these words with us. In a way that you don't quite accept yet, this book is being brought to you by "All That Is" in a loving and caring framework you will understand. The occasional humor and personality bleed-throughs are portions of "All That Is" closer to you, acting as intermediaries you might say, but still larger portions of yourself. This is a cooperative venture, as you know, and much coordination goes into these pages.

(1) THE SEEDING OF THE PHYSICAL UNIVERSE:

Given the simultaneous nature of time, was our world truly "seeded" as suggested here?

Yes and no. Your universe is being constantly created in the context of the eternal now, yet within the **flexibility of time** itself there is ample room for genetic experimentation and playing with value fulfillment. It is in this arena that there are numerous experiments taking place with varying combinations of physical senses, intuitive discernment and a blending of the two.

The confusion here can be rectified with an understanding of time as a rich medium that allows for an unlimited degree of flexibility within the eternal now. While it is true that there is no "past" or "future" in a more expansive definition of time, there is a stepping outside of time altogether and "playing" with these concepts. This is an area that could fill an entire volume – "The Nature of Time in the Context of the Eternal Now".

• • •

LESSON (32), NOVEMBER 29, 1987

The implementation of these concepts into terms that can be translated into **physical success** will require practice of the exercises we are giving you. For your readers who take this writing seriously, a glance at the Seth material(1) may be helpful for prerequisite understanding of those concepts that won't be fully discussed in these pages. This is not absolutely necessary, but it will help if these concepts are to be carried forward to the degree necessary for the successful completion of mind over matter manipulations and the implosion of neutrons mentioned earlier. Further, an understanding of the illusionary aspects of your physical plane is absolutely necessary, and having an emotional understanding in the form of subsequent experience(2) will be most helpful.

(1) COMMENT ON THE SETH/JANE ROBERTS BOOKS:

For those who are interested, I feel that "Seth Speaks" provides the best overview of the entire collection of Jane Roberts' books. "The Nature of Personal Reality" is a "handbook" for knowing yourself and making desired changes in your life – and chapter 10 of "The Seth Material" offers an understanding of the illusionary aspects of our physical reality.

(2) COMMENT:

The "experience" referred to here represents a feel for the illusionary quality of our reality. This feeling will follow upon the merging of intellectual understanding and practice of the exercises.

A breakthrough will occur for each reader at his or her own pace and commitment.

● ● ●

LESSON (33), NOVEMBER 29, 1987

The implementation of the processes outlined will occur in spurts of success that will build one onto the next breakthrough. Your ability to concentrate on your given image is, as mentioned earlier, a prerequisite to further experimentation. After the ability to hold your image has been perfected, you will be able to direct these images into desired ends which will affect your physical field. The intensity of your visualization will hasten the progress of these exercises, but for the time being, simply practice your ability to hold your image. When we progress with further understandings of the "powers of visualization", you will be amazed as to what can be accomplished. We hesitate to overuse the word "visualization" in these exercises because the concept has become commonplace in your literature and perhaps somewhat trite – but it has unlimited potential that cannot be minimized.

What we are stressing, as you might suspect, is a method of **empowering your visualization** abilities by a "knowing" that you are all Gods. And that your abilities are a gift from "All That Is", imparted onto all of you in the simultaneous creation of all realities that you are obviously a part of and one with. When you **accept your divinity** you will have no difficulty accepting the abilities inherent in your genes and in your imagination, which is behind the creation of your physical worlds as much as any creator outside of your perception. It is this union and ONENESS that we are trying to impart into your knowing, in terms that you will accept. To the extent we are successful in convincing you of your oneness, the sooner these concepts will gel and make enough sense to you to give you the impetus and courage to prove to yourselves that these aren't merely theories.

You do indeed have the ability to communicate with your atomic particles and direct their thrust into directions of a most creative nature. This knowing will provide you with a power source so awesome that it will negate any sense of shortage or limitation that you are currently allowing yourselves to dictate your thinking. Your world was meant to be self-sufficient, and it will be as soon as you see yourselves as unlimited – which you are!

• • •

LESSON (34), NOVEMBER 30, 1987

The power of **one successful neutron implosion** is literally enough to power an average city of 400,000 people for several hours – and this can be accomplished in individual terms by anyone proficient in the visualization process required. When groups of people are considered in a directed manner, this effect is of course magnified many times. Here we are talking of a city's power needs being satisfied for the entire year. And with only the combined efforts of a dozen individuals and simple mechanical apparatus, you will be able to store and further direct and define this energy for more specifically measured needs, i.e. automobiles, heat and general power needs, limited only by your imagination and further technological developments.

It might seem ludicrous to you at this stage to picture yourselves moving from the simple meditation practice of holding an image – to the implementation of the power supply we speak of. That gap, however, will be crossed with the speed of your intent and abilities being built up to necessary intensities.

The mechanical aspects of our model are secondary and will be discussed in later lessons. The idea of storing this individual or group induced energy will be the **transmission phase,** as you conceive of a transmission in an automobile. The major difference, of course, is that in your automobile the differential is driven by the internal combustion engine which has proven to be quite the "workhorse" since your industrial revolution. It is now polluting your environment to quite unnecessary degrees, however, and will prove to be rather limiting in the decades to follow. We are not suggesting that this will occur immediately, for that would cause unnecessary trauma to your world economies. What we are suggesting is that once accepted and understood, our model will gradually **replace your dependence on fossil fuels.**

More importantly, it will completely negate the need for your primitive atomic powerhouses which are ticking time bombs in terms of potential disasters, and certain eventual problems of varying magnitude with regard to the disposal of your radioactive wastes. We are talking of future generations as well as those of you who will be around at the turn of the century. With regard to your **nuclear warheads,** we will not tolerate their deployment(1), but would rather not intervene if it can be avoided. We are rather amused at the stockpile of weapons of this nature in the name of peace. We are also impressed with the fact that you have not deployed more of these weapons than you have, which certainly does show a compassion that was lacking just a few centuries ago.

(1) QUESTION:

Do I take your statement literally that you will not allow the deployment of our nuclear missiles?

Yes, Michael, even though you may interpret this as interference in the free will your plane. You are not alone in the universe, and the pollution of your atmosphere goes beyond the limits of your space as you understand it. It would interfere with probabilities of those not on a collision course. **Free-will** here requires a much larger perspective. Your unwillingness to come to terms with your creative abilities in a peaceful and cooperative manner shall not interfere with those planes where these issues have been dealt with.

● ● ●

LESSON (35), DECEMBER 1, 1987

The speed of electrons can seem baffling to your perspective of relative motion, and the solid appearance of your matter can seem equally baffling taking into consideration that there appears to be nothing solid about your atoms in the first place. When considering that the space between your electrons spinning around the nucleus leaves vast amounts of space in between, you have a giant vacuum that now appears to comprise your physical structures. It becomes believable, of course, because of your intent to operate in a physical medium which offers opportunities for growth in ways quite impossible otherwise. Now, even in physical terms, your reality can be seen as illusionary – and before we are finished we hope to assure you that even though there are obviously illusionary aspects of your world, "you" are not an illusion. You are vital powerhouses of probabilities, capable of far more creativity than you have previously imagined.

One of our aims is to stretch your imagination to incorporate the vast potential that lies within the **manipulation of your chosen illusion.** It is not physical to us, so this becomes rather academic from our perspective. We realize that since you don't currently have our perspective this can seem rather unsettling to you. The gap between your reality and ours in obvious terms is the very fact that we are not physical beings and choose not to view reality through physical senses as you do with your focus. When you learn that you have other senses equally valid, you will realize that there is far more reality to be perceived than the physical field that seems to surround you.

● ● ●

LESSON (36), DECEMBER 2, 1987

The bringing together and implementation of the theories we have proposed dealing with a self-generating energy source will require **a reshaping of your self-image** toward the realization that you are all Gods, and as such, capable of simulating the creative process. This goes beyond the imagination exercises required, because it is mimicking a trust that you haven't quite accepted. There is nothing esoteric about our model, and its implementation will serve you on many levels beyond the obvious. It will act as an integration of a most multidimensional nature since it will bring your people together in a cooperative venture that will enhance personal power, group potential, unleash energy beyond your wildest dreams – **and** get you in touch with your ONENESS with the creation and the creator.

This will in turn lead to numerous other fulfillments, the probabilities of which have not even emerged in the realm of your imagination. You are leading into an age of rapid change and an exciting one for those who wish to participate in the awesome growth potential it offers. There is much excitement in our realm, and a great gathering of energies going into your metamorphosis.

"You are self-sufficient . . . you all came into your world with all you needed to carry on your challenges . . ."

Chapter Eight

MOBILITY OF CONSCIOUSNESS

LESSON (37), DECEMBER 3, 1987

The employment of mental process into physical change involves a crossing point of thought into energy and form. Thought and form **are** energy, so the transition is a natural one. The only re-arranging required are your thoughts, because **thought is the entire process** and building block. Directed thought into channels that intersect with coordinate points at designated angles greatly enhances the manifestation process. Here you are literally **bending energy into your intent.** The process we will describe is not altogether foreign to you since you do it all the time, but unconsciously. We are bringing your subconscious process here into your conscious awareness so as to give you greater flexibility and adaptability for desired ends.

As previously stated, we will give you various symbols to place in schematic form on the contours of your mind to be visualized for "re-creation of the creative process". The symbols can be put into chart form, and through reflection, be translated into a useable format. **Our first symbol is a** 🜔 and reflects a bend in energy that transcends a sense of **double space** or space folding in onto itself. This process adds tremendous leverage to the formulation of intensities necessary for further deployment into our next step.

• • •

LESSON (38), DECEMBER 4, 1987

We will name these symbols as we proceed, but names as you know, are merely for convenience. We will establish solid footing first. The symbols you are receiving are **suggested tools** that will greatly enhance your creative abilities in a demonstrable form, which will be so important initially. Once you have become comfortable with the group of exercises you are receiving, utilizing the **bends in thought** required for each, you will have a feel for what we are getting at. The next symbol is **J** , similar to your letter "J" and an **ᒐ** , a reversed letter "J". These appear horizontally on your page, even though we mean to imply an inward or outward projection of thought accompanied by an upward thrust as seen by these symbols.

In time, you will have **mechanical devices** that will simulate these motions for you. Similar to your biofeedback machines, they will help train your technicians in a rather simplified manner. Once these maneuvers are made second nature, you will be able to manipulate in your physical field with small objects at first, but in a manner that will build up to greater and greater potential. We will introduce mechanical devices to further enhance the required mental process that will enable you to establish the "circuits of intent" we have spoken of.

● ● ●

LESSON (39), DECEMBER 4, 1987

The progression of symbols we are introducing don't necessarily imply any order of difficulty or importance. They are all important and some will be easier than others to master, but all are quite within your grasp. Collectively, they will impart an **inner mosaic of thought**(1) and a sense of directed energy onto the recesses of your mind that you will be able to access when needed. We will separate thought and energy for convenience, but know that as "time and space", they are one. The revelations that will flow from this understanding offers tremendous potential in the form of added leverage.

Our next symbol is a **O** , replicating your zero or letter "O", implying a circular motion at varying angles. We will designate these angles with yet another set of symbols. This will be the most nebulous of the symbols since it will encompass various **intensities and angles.** Angles here don't imply intersections, but rather designated spatial relationships to **fixed postures** within your mosaic. We will explain postures as varying perspectives within the given circuit that will allow for pausing and further projection. The process will first have to be understood on mental and experiential levels before you can "program" your mechanical devices – that will in time save energy and transmission procedures.

(1) INNER MOSAIC OF THOUGHT:

We have been taught to associate with our outer or physical senses, i.e. sight, sound, smell, touch and taste. The psychological counterpart of our outer senses would be our inner senses – the workshop of our mind. It is the inner senses that are being appealed to here, and the inner mosaic of thought are mental pathways or "inner maps" that can be created and recalled at will.

• • •

LESSON (40), DECEMBER 5, 1987

The motion of energy as you direct your thought through these exercises will move precisely in the lines of your intent. The clearer your intent, focus and understanding of process, the greater your leverage. Concentration is so important here to maximize the thrust of your thought as it impinges on designated angles of coordinate points that you will learn to recognize. The points of energy you are working with are "awarized", and as such, will play along with you if you allow it. **Moving into and directing this flow is the objective.** The symbols are tools to help you maneuver in and out of directed exercises and maximize the utility of your creative powers to meet your desired ends.

The clarity and intensity of your emotions here are synonymous with "our" directed thought, the difference being that on our plane we are quite consciously acting in orchestration with creative processes that ordinarily you have kept at subconscious levels. The next symbol is a ⟲ , similar to your letter "Z". This involves directing thought outwardly and inwardly in a downward swivel following the pattern of our ⟲ . All of these patterns can be utilized from different angles for different results, and there will be subvalues to help implement these intended angles.

• • •

LESSON (41), DECEMBER 6, 1987

The collection of symbols represent tools to be utilized in the exercises that will follow. To become proficient, you must practice, as in any endeavor. **Everyone is capable of success to some degree,** dependent on intent. Those who take these concepts seriously and make the necessary commitment to understand the prerequisite considerations behind these exercises will be awed by the power inherent in their thought. This can start as an amusing game to merely challenge your curiosity. However, when various degrees of success **are** reached, perhaps you will gain the impetus to take these concepts a bit more seriously. They are meant for everyone, even though many will obviously not read these pages. Enough of you will, however, to get the ball rolling and generate ever increasing momentum to chart a unified front.

When some of your scientists begin experimenting with thought and scholarly papers are introduced to doubting journals, there will be funding made available for further study by some surprising sources. The concepts we introduced underlying the exercises can be found in many popular books of the 1980's dealing with "channeled" material. We are simply introducing them in ways that augment the mental process that is the crux of our model. The next symbol is ⌐_ , or simply right angles as seen from different perspectives. These can be adapted to sharper angles **L ➤** , etc. and the "0's" can be interconnected as **⚛** . Additional symbols aren't necessary at this time, and the next step in our series of exercises is practicing one symbol at a time until you are comfortable with visualizing your thoughts at these directed angles, formations and postures.

• • •

LESSON (42), DECEMBER 7, 1987

Movement into the flow that you are questioning is accomplished through intent. Once achieved, you do indeed have a new gestalt of awarized energy with "its" intent now considered. Because it was **your** intent that set up this gestalt, you have an amazing degree of control over the overall interaction of this energy's thrust into your specified objective.

It will help to consider your new gestalt as an "awarized thrust" of thought controlled energy that has power beyond your normal range of frequency and concentration. It has merged with you for the purpose of blending space/time into your direction for your designated objective. As awarized, however, it takes your intent further into the reaches of space/time than you are consciously aware of.

It is almost as though this gestalt has a mind of its own, and as such, will impinge into probabilities that don't have to concern you now. But know that your intent and awarized gestalt are quite multidimensional and have far reaching effects in a multitude of realities. Not only can you use this gestalt to act on your behalf through your intent, but you are creating a new combination of energy for purposes that go beyond your objective for "others" to ponder. This becomes a new direction for further study once understood.

• • •

LESSON (43), DECEMBER 8, 1987

The transition of thought into observable effect will take on a marked improvement by anyone developing the proficiency at concentration and mobility abilities. The first step is accepting the premise that it is possible, and the second is having the faith that you are capable of unleashing your own energies. There is **no secret to this approach,** only an ever increasing understanding of your awesome power that you have until now placed outside of yourselves. We are simply telling you that that which seems to be outside of yourselves is your projection of thought into a picture of a world that you call reality.

The only reality of substance is the reality of your mind! Until you explore your inner pathways, you will continue to believe in the "dualities"(1) of your world that place you outside of nature, god, and even yourselves. You see a difference between mind and body, mind and the outside world. These dualities served a purpose as your race was experimenting with ego development at a time when your ego was critical in survival terms. This is no longer necessary, however, and you are capable of a much larger perspective of your connectedness and subsequent power that is waiting to be acknowledged. Life can be infinitely more spontaneous and fulfilling once you understand your part in nature, and stop thinking in terms of survival of the fittest(2) and each man for himself. An infinitely more cooperative perspective is possible and necessary if your race is to flourish along lines of your potential.

(1) DUALITIES:

The concept of dualities rests on the belief in an exteriorized world and the logic of opposites. It is assumed that we are separate from our environment. If there is good, there must be evil, our world is positive & negative, ying & yang. Once we accept that there is nothing "outside" of God and nothing outside of ourselves but projection, there becomes no need to entertain endless separations.

While dualities and seeming opposites appear to make obvious sense, when a larger picture of reality is observed, a unity of opposites and a sense of connectedness prevails. Accomplishing this merging requires an expansion of one-dimensional thinking.

(2) SURVIVAL OF THE FITTEST:

While denying the animal kingdom a worthwhile or blessed consciousness, **Charles Darwin** projected onto the animals "mans" worst behavior. This was a reversal of mans own perceived struggle for survival that he placed on the animals themselves – which he had no right to conclude[1]. His categorizing and objectifying the various species blinded him to the inner balances of nature and the overall cooperativeness of the animals and their environment. This created a pattern of thinking that has persisted.

Evidence of the miraculous interdependence and cooperation of nature is too often taken for granted. How each facet fits in so perfectly with each other, and how each exists for the well-being of the whole, is an awesome balance to behold. Every animal has its own biological integrity which escapes us when we approach our observation in a "scientific" manner.

When one animal kills another for food, the "victim", even while appearing frightened, accepts its fate and recognizes its inviolate nature and survival in basic terms. As long as man refuses to relate to the animal kingdom in "emotional" terms, he misses out on this biological splendor and cooperation that is everywhere apparent. The proof of this cooperation lies in our own personal and emotional experience, an area that science considers outside of its concern.

1- "The Afterdeath Journal of an American Philosopher – The World View of William James" by Jane Roberts. Chapter 4

"Within the circumstances you find yourselves, you all have the ability to learn who you are — and this becomes the only lesson that ultimately matters."

Chapter Nine

THOUGHT-FORMS

LESSON (44), DECEMBER 9, 1987

Circuits of intent will be utilized for either manifestation purposes or the release of energy potential inherent in the process itself. You can liken these circuits to the concept of thought-forms that you are already familiar with. **Thought-forms** are a part of your everyday reality as much as your breathing. They basically involve directed thought into any given area, whether conscious constructions, visualization, or daydreaming.

Whenever you gather your energies and concentrate along lines of a given intent, you are creating a thought-form that does not dissipate as you change the pattern of your thought. It goes on to create other worlds(1) that need not concern our discussion. What does concern you is your conscious ability to create thought-forms that can be most powerful as a stimulus to create change or release energy – and gather further energy by others as they join in your construction along the lines of similar intent. As individuals, you can imagine a joint effort in your thought-form constructions which can add considerably to the force of those constructions.

The object here is to **objectify** these thought-forms in a manner that is observable to you in terms of understanding their power and flexibility of purpose. Our next exercise will be one of developing a feel for thought construction, and the form and pattern they take in mental terms prior to manifestation phases. This will be another visualization process, and one of a most beneficial nature. You will learn to **outline the object of your intent,** observing and sensing your thought as it translates into intensities that will affect your physical plane.

(1) MERGING WITH MY SOUL ESSENCE:

The concept of our thoughts and emotions creating other worlds has always fascinated me. This is tied into an incident that occurred in 1982 after an intense emotional encounter. I spontaneously picked up "Seth Speaks" as a diversion and randomly began reading a line asking ". . . what happens to a thought after it leaves your awareness?" I had read this passage several times before and thought it was an unachievable exercise. This time, however, I didn't question the possibility of the challenge.

Focusing on a footstool, I closed my eyes and as the object began to wander, I mentally followed it. I found myself spontaneously projecting my consciousness seemingly into the future after a tremendous acceleration. What transpired was one of the most amazing experiences of my life during which time I shared the perspective of my greater self for about five minutes – which had no counterpart in time. Taken from my notes written down after that experience . . .

"I found myself in an ocean of consciousness with no barriers of time or space. It was an awesome sense of pure knowing propelled by the loving connectedness of my greater self. There was the tremendous presence of my entity – affectionate, caring, and utterly familiar. It was a different part of "me", inseparable and difficult to distinguish where we merged. It was as though a puzzle had just been completed for the first time in my conscious memory. I was in awe of how powerful I was and have always been! In a most dramatic way, I came to understand that I didn't "have" a soul, I **am** my soul!

I sensed the absolute ONENESS between every aspect of All That Is, with the very "space" that surrounded me filled with the same vitality of creation. There was a feeling of freedom, completeness and absolute safety, with an overwhelming sense of **love as the medium.** This "love" permeated every thought and every aspect of my perspective. There was no empty space, but an "atmospheric presence" that connected me with every other facet of godhood that I could comprehend. My potential and connectedness was unbounded.

There were many entities in the vicinity, but I was too overwhelmed to focus on anything but the euphoria that enraptured me. There was no "outside" to my divinity and I knew that the universe had always been supportive of me and everybody else at the same time. All of the anxieties that had plagued me while in my body were made so insignificant knowing of my oneness with "source". There was tremendous purpose and importance for all of my desires, and everyone elses as they merged into the gestalt of my surroundings.

As I found myself projecting back to my body awareness, I didn't want to leave that indescribable emotional richness. Asking if I could stay, I felt a cosmic laughter and an unforgettable sense of "recklessness". It was a multidimensional reminder not to take life overly serious. I could never view my physical focus quite the same, sensing the infinite support in every action of every moment. The most mundane of activity was blessed. There was nothing to fear about life **or** death! Death was nothing less than an indescribable transition and return to the yearnings of my psyche."

• • •

LESSON (45), DECEMBER 9, 1987

Thought-forms, as you understand them, are gestalts of awarized energy reflecting the imagination of the sender. Know that this gestalt of energy becomes inviolate in certain terms and has power to a relative degree "independent" of the sender. The forms are composed of thought/energy, and as such, contain the same units of consciousness as appear in all realities, whether physically perceived or not.

In basic terms, your planet is a thought-form agreed upon by all its inhabitants. Because of the degree of participation, you might say, your earth takes on characteristics of a most believable thought-form – although the perspective and value fulfillment of the flora, fauna and so-called inanimate objects, differ widely. The point being, that individually you are capable of creating thought-forms of a most beneficial and healing nature – and collectively, you are capable of thought-forms powerful enough to move mountains, quite literally! As individuals accept and appreciate the power of their thought, you will have a power supply of a self-generating nature that will carry you beyond your current concepts of cooperation.

● ● ●

LESSON (46), DECEMBER 10, 1987

Power, as you have been taught to understand, is one force acting upon another. This is distorted in a very basic manner and we wish to address the issue. Power is always a relative term, but "power of" is clearer than "power over". Power over implies that something or someone is more powerful than the object of the takeover. There is relative power to the degree of imagination of any given energy/personality, but it is **limited only by the extent of knowing.** An important issue is unraveling here, namely that "all" have the same inherent power since it is the **power of being!** This implies an integrity and inviolate power of awesome proportion. It implies a model of "All That Is" in probabilities and potential in a most unified manner and in a way that makes "power over" meaningless.

We are one, seemingly separated for dualities of experience, to better know ourselves and return to the conclusion that we indeed are one – and in that knowing we become greater than that who wondered what could be learned by these experiments of duality. We never stop wondering and we never cease to be awed by our power to create, as we have been created. There are intimate connections here between creation, imagination and thought – and our ability to manifest beyond any boundaries, since boundaries are only temporary pauses in our knowing(1).

(1) BOUNDARIES:

Boundaries can be likened to separation, dualities, cause and effect, or any sense of opposites that in greater terms are artificial. From the perspective of "All That Is" there are no boundaries – yet to emerging consciousnesses such as ourselves, boundaries are ever present. They help us differentiate experience in order to help us grow in an orderly fashion. As we move into higher or finer vibrational planes, boundaries would become less and less apparent. In these terms, our world is a training ground for a time when we will be able to operate in a "boundless" environment.

● ● ●

LESSON (47), DECEMBER 11, 1987

The impetus to share our awareness with you comes at a time when your planet is indeed undergoing an acceleration of knowing and a stepping aside from beliefs that have separated you from an understanding of who you are. Who you are and who we are is a moot point, since we are aspects of each other currently choosing to experience reality from different perspectives. We can impart our awareness onto you for manipulation of your physical reality up to a point. We cannot and have no intention of undermining your root assumptions and mass hallucination(1). You can, however, make great strides in understanding who you are and what you are capable of – and in so doing, break down barriers that separate your reality from ours.

There is **much leeway between nonphysical and physical realities** in terms of experimentation that can utilize the basic knowing that we are all gods and all one. To the degree that this is understood, your planet will undergo an acceleration of a most positive nature in terms of harmony and self-sufficiency. It's a knowing that you **are** self-sufficient, and that you all came into your world with all you needed to carry on your challenges in terms of the value fulfillment chosen. Within the circumstance you find yourselves, you all have the ability to learn who you are – and this becomes the only lesson that ultimately matters.

(1) MASS HALLUCINATION:

This perhaps is an unsettling way of describing our reality, yet the fact remains that our focus only appears physical to those consciousnesses taking part in our grand play. When an "alien" personality looks in on our world, it is indeed hallucinatory in nature until our space/time vibration is accessed. Viewing our reality in this manner can also give us an appreciation for our dream state, which in greater terms is no more hallucinatory than our waking state. Likewise, our thoughts become as valid as our physical perspective!

Chapter Ten

A UNIFIED FIELD OF THOUGHT

LESSON (48), DECEMBER 12, 1987

Thought-form construction is accomplished quite effortlessly on a subconscious level in a way that creates your physical world in the first place. Your world is being created continuously by all of its inhabitants and collectively you agree on its validity. When enough participants of your world understand the nature of physical reality, you will make great strides in your abilities to change it. This implies working with your environment in a cooperative venture, because you will sense how you are connected to each other and to your planet. This knowing has already begun. Our intent is to add to your awareness and abilities that go along with that knowing.

The power of thought can never be minimized, and you are first beginning to appreciate that power on conscious terms. We will attempt to identify for you certain phases you all go through in the **process of thought construction** – and encourage you to develop a feel for each stage so as to be able to accentuate and empower the direction of your thought.

It appears to you that your thoughts just appear and then disappear. You are sensing your thought here from a very limited perspective. There is a **unified field of thought**(1) that takes into consideration your entire planet and beyond, but you are simply tuning into those bands that can be translated by your given physical senses. As you learn to expand your senses to include quite valid inner senses, you will learn to recognize entirely **new bands of thought** that you previously were tuning out. This will be a major awakening for many as you begin to access and interpret thought that doesn't seem to fit in with your current concepts of reality.

The origination of your thoughts(2) are tied in with this unified field in a way that keeps you quite abreast on current events as to the conditions and circumstances of your planet at any given time. This field offers vast potential in terms of understanding and implementing a power source that will be unleashed as soon as you gain sufficient expertise at accessing the required vibration. The concentration and mobility of thought exercises will be helpful in enabling you to handle the intensity of these energies, and once accomplished, you will have access to a **power of unlimited degree** at your disposal at all times. It is toward this end we challenge you(3) at this time.

(1) UNIFIED FIELD OF THOUGHT:

Within the consciousnesses of the varying participants of our planet, there is an instinctive understanding of the **connectedness** between all species and their environment. The extent to which this connectedness is interpreted will vary from species to species, but man is perhaps the most distant from this awareness. The rose has a keen appreciation of its surroundings (mentioned in Lesson 7), but man, because of his particular ego development, has chosen to ignore this unity. The plants and animals would interpret the unified field as part of their awareness that needs no definition. They understand their oneness in these terms and are aware of planetary communication in a way that we are just beginning to appreciate.

(2) ORIGINATION OF THOUGHT:

If we consider the collective consciousness as a global conversation taking place between all aspects of our planet, the origination of thought becomes our intent to communicate with the particular band we wish to entertain. There is no origin as such, but the freedom to initiate a new connection or path. This is tied in with the original creation and "All That Is" expressing and searching for more of itself in a simultaneous never ending creative expansion.

(3) COLLECTIVE CHALLENGE:

Because of our intense focus on objectivity in recent centuries, we have often ignored the potentials of intuition and imagination. There are many inhabited planets where the personalities involved are exploring a radically different path. Rather than a developing belief in the physical properties of their surroundings, many of these planes have focused on consciousness itself and how it creates and colors their perception.

In this manner, there has been no perceived need to be as creative in outward terms, but rather in the workshop of the mind. Whereas we assume that our mechanical devices must be physically operative to be useful, in these experiments, they are mentally tested first and explored in expansive "inner terms". A merging of this potential with our current insistence on objectivity becomes one of the next concepts to be explored in terms of earth change.

Nikola Tesla played with these concepts relative to how he mentally perfected his discoveries before ever creating a working model. His perspective was radically different than most scientists, and his achievements were most prolific as a result (discussed in Lesson 27, 83, and the appendices).

● ● ●

LESSON (49), DECEMBER 13, 1987

The unified field of thought is not as mystical as it might sound. If you consider the entire planet as having **a group mind** and each individual simply tuning into the conversation that interests each of them, you can begin to understand the concept. It goes much beyond that, of course, since each inhabitant initiates his or her individual version of thought, as well as the animals, plants, rocks, soil, oceans, insects, etc. - all of which have their input into this group mind. Every "thought" that originates from any of these sources changes and affects all other thought to a degree and a "ripple affect" is created that affects the entire planet.

Thought not only connects you to each other, but to all other realities as well. The intensity of your thought has much to say about the considered acknowledgement and reply. Now this explanation doesn't tell you where anyone or "anything's" thought originates – this takes yet another explanation. The physical world you relate to is being created continuously, and as such, it helps to consider time as being simultaneous in the context of an **eternal now.** Within that eternal now a constant creation makes sense, as well as the concepts of infinity and God. Since creation is constantly and simultaneously occurring, **the origin of your thoughts is none other than "All That Is"** manifesting all realities in an **explosion of being!**

This doesn't imply any connection with your big bang theory popular with some of your physicists, but with a primordial spontaneous "letting go" where All That Is could no longer contain the images of what it felt it could manifest. Potentials would have been lost that are implied in none other than yourselves, since you are literally part of and models of "All That Is". We are dealing with concepts that are most difficult to place in linear terms and into a vocabulary that lacks words that could imply the full thrust of creation that you are a part of. Know that you have been created from this original explosion of being, and that you dwell in the loving thrust of an eternal validity and a most marvelous multidimensional connectedness that you are just beginning to glimpse.

● ● ●

LESSON (50), DECEMBER 14, 1987

We wish to review a few basic points at this time. Your physical world as you know it is an illusion, and it is through this illusion that you judge all aspects of reality. The tricky part of this method is that it becomes difficult to **determine origins** or boundaries since you are continuously defining and redefining smaller and smaller aspects of matter and models of the mind as it relates to human behavior. If you would step aside for a moment and recognize that your particles of matter are coagulated thought-forms and that there is indeed an inseparable link between mind and matter, you would be taking a giant step in the right direction.

Further understand that consciousness is and always has been at the gates of all creation. There was no time when consciousness and awareness weren't part of the total universe. **Consciousness creates form**(1), not the other way around. Once these concepts are understood, we can move on to areas that might still be received with a bit of doubt since you are not convinced yet of the awesome power that lies within your mental ability.

The circuits of intent will be the basic method through which we would like you to develop an understanding and become comfortable with on individual levels. You can all start by making the necessary **commitment to practice** the concentration and mobility of consciousness exercises. When you become proficient at these, you will automatically attract the energy necessary to carry you further into the intensities required to manipulate your physical field to varying degrees.

The energy we are talking about is already in and around the aura of your earth, as you experienced in your "telephone out-of-body experience" with your friend Beth (mentioned in the Introduction). It is precisely this energy that will be descending onto your plane as you move into your new age. The exercises, if done in a disciplined manner, will go a long way in helping you direct this energy once you become aware of it(2).

The energy will at first be attracted to those who are in a position to utilize and direct it in a conscious manner. It will eventually be apparent throughout your lands, and to some, will appear quite overwhelming. There is no "danger" as such connected with this vibration, only ignorance and fear. This wave of energy comes at a time when your planet will be shifting into a **faster vibrational sphere** where manifestation and energy transformation will become second nature. For those of you who don't wish to accept this challenge, you will have several choices(3) – but the easiest, as will become apparent, will be to acknowledge, accept, and learn to assimilate with it. It will be a true joy to those who don't fight it, for they will sense their godhood and connectedness in a much more directed and obvious manner.

This vibration will carry along with it abilities that you have long forgotten, as well as a knowing that you are all gods. There is great potential here to **unify your planet** to a degree unheard of in present culture. The general mood will be ripe for taking the step into the acknowledgements and awareness we are imparting on you as these shifts begin to take place. We are not speaking of a shift in the axis of your physical planet, but rather a shift in vibrational frequency that will carry you into the arena of your divinity with far less effort than you currently imagine.

(1) CONSCIOUSNESS & CREATION:

Creation did not arise from from the "big bang" as some scientists would consider, but from an explosion of being in conscious terms. "Before" this creation, there was consciousness that was becoming more and more aware of itself. It becomes limiting to ask "when was the beginning", since the "beginning" had no relevance to time as we understand it. Time was created as a means to explore this creation in cause and effect fashion, but can't be used to gauge events outside of our reality continuum. We step into time and out of time continuously, but are usually unaware of the transition.

(2) EXPERIENCING THE FOURTH DIMENSION:

When and if we will experience this vibration becomes a matter of faith. When I experienced it as an initiation to this manuscript, it was a multidimensional, unbelievably powerful and emotionally rich encounter that left me breathless!

(3) CHOICES & THE NEW AGE:

As we move more and more into the momentum of earth change, it will become clear that the basic emotional choices are:

a) Clarity of thought and accessibility of self:

Emotional openness and honesty with ourselves, recognizing the tremendous inner support that becomes available . . .

(or)

b) Holding on to separation and limitation:

Emotional rigidity and fear that binds us to belief patterns telling us that we are unworthy or fearful of our own potential. This choice will become more and more difficult to sustain.

In terms of those who choose not to maintain their physical focus on earth, they will have many more paths open to them than in previous incarnations. There are many probabilities opening up to help these individuals accept the fourth dimension at their own pace on parallel universes very similar to our own. Many of these people will not even be aware of the transition. Much of my recent channeling has dealt with these issues, and will be incorporated in future books.

● ● ●

LESSON (51), DECEMBER 15, 1987

Acting on behalf of yourselves first is the only way to proceed, for if you haven't come to terms with your own energy, you can't very well help others. This is true in general terms as well as the upcoming vibrational shift. Many "new age" books go into great detail outlining various approaches that can help you sort out your thoughts and beliefs in the context of knowing yourselves better, as well as outlining the nature of reality from differing viewpoints. We are not dealing with these issues as such, but rather with being aware of the inherent power of **directing your thought** in lines of intent to help you assimilate the faster vibration that will be so very apparent within many of your lifetimes.

Once again, the **time frame** of these changes will not be the same for everyone, but your planet will be affected in an increasingly noticeable manner beginning in the coming decade of your time (the 1990's). By the turn of the century, you will have a noticeable shift in priorities on a global scale, moving away from political extremes into a realization that you have a common goal to work towards – one that will require a balance of politics and economics with a rethinking of your religious doctrines as well.

As a clearer perspective on the nature of your physical world becomes more apparent, your many and varied institutions will begin to bend to accommodate these new awarenesses. This won't happen at once, of course, but in a process that will be in full swing by the year 2020. These time frames aren't cast in stone but represent probabilities that at the moment look rather determined. We don't mean to imply that you will have a utopia in short order, but that the vibrational shift we speak of will have been set in motion to a point where it will be quite apparent throughout your planet by that year. The majority of your population will accept these changes with some confusion, but enough of you will be in a position to understand these happenings to help maintain relative order.

The part nature has to play will depend upon how well this transformation takes place, i.e. the more resistance, the more apparent shifts in weather patterns and various storms, earthquakes, floods, etc. Weather patterns have always been a function of emotional state(1), but now the connection will become more and more apparent. So will the inadequacy of your models of self defense, political boundaries, economic institutions, etc. It is not that these will collapse as such, but that they will have to be reshaped to accommodate a cooperative venture that you have not yet had to deal with.

We are not suggesting a global disaster or anarchy, but a **re-alignment of priorities** to accommodate a knowing that you are all one with yourselves and your surroundings. To the degree that you come to terms with the power implied in these shifts and are able to move from the understanding of an external power to one quite contained within your selfhood, you will make the transition much smoother for yourself and those around you.

(1) EMOTIONAL STATES & WEATHER PATTERNS:

A wide range of consciousness on our planet releases electromagnetic properties as a result of varying emotional states. This release of emotion, in collective terms, will have its effect on the atmosphere of a given area. Consider the human body as it gives off adrenaline when highly excited. This reaction affects the "extended body" as well and has its affect on nearby weather patterns. When considering a highly charged area of the collective consciousness, storms are as much emotional as they are "atmospheric".

Natural disasters such as earthquakes and floods do not reflect "random" reactions of nature – but rather a collective response of the "extended body" to express itself and balance the organism. Our exterior world will always be a perfect reflection of our interior condition at any given time. This is true in personal terms as well as in overall global terms. Extreme weather conditions will become more and more apparent to coincide with the great social changes that will accompany our general earth changes.

The consciousness of the earth itself has not been appreciated in recent history. When man separated himself from nature, the integrity of the planet was lost. Earth is a living, breathing, viable organism that is aware of itself in greater conscious terms than we have collectively chosen to acknowledge. At any point of extreme danger, the earth will shake itself free of that danger. This effect will be magnified in the coming decades in the most humane way the planet has of "healing itself".

"Your reality maintains its appearance only to those who wish to participate in it."

Chapter Eleven

A VIBRATIONAL SHIFT

LESSON (52), DECEMBER 16, 1987

A **utopia** where political and economic differences have been worked out and where there are no basic inequalities in the division of natural resources sounds very evocative indeed. The truest and most ideal utopia, of course, is where each person has the blessing and support to walk through life knowing that he is free and has the support to work toward the potential he senses individually and in terms of how he feels he can contribute to his world.

There are **many inhabited planets** in your physical galaxy, as well as in other probabilities and galaxies beyond your concepts of space. The type of utopia we speak of is apparent to a relative degree in all realities of a physical nature, although as you might suspect, most realities aren't physical in the way you understand them. There are many possibilities here of worlds that would seem not to have physical qualities, but where the inhabitants have the ability to manifest physically at their discretion. The reason for these evolutionary experiments are no different than your own – simply in keeping with a program of self-discovery, utilizing an imaginative mixture of root assumptions and value fulfillment.

In the totality of universal perspective, **your plane is a relatively primitive one**(1), with no judgement implied. Within your beings, you all have the capacity to know who you are, and as a result, live up to your potentials. One of our main objectives here is to help you along in understanding those potentials, and introduce you to the upcoming changes on your plane in such a way that will give you a glimpse of what you can expect. We are not being overly specific for a very good reason. You all have **free-will,** and as such, leave open many possibilities as to how the earth changes will transpire.

How the planet is affected in geographic terms is left open, although it does appear that there could be some major shifts in land masses at the worst end of probabilities – and at the best, a relatively smooth transition where loss of life is still inevitable, but so is it currently with your constant skirmishes. It is not that simple of course, since we are dealing with varying **probabilities(2)** within the probable earth you are a part of.

Without getting overly complicated, your earth will be a different place for different individuals since each of you will **meet the environment of your intent.** It could be said that you have numerous paths that will all be explored, and to the individuals involved in each, he or she may not even be aware of those other paths. The whole area of probabilities can be fascinating discussion, but not in the framework of this particular work. The point we wish to make, however, is that through the changes that will be taking place on your planet, you will be more in line with your potential as a people and more on a par with your galactic neighbors.

(1) EARTH & UNIVERSAL PERSPECTIVE:

In basic terms, comparison of awareness is getting into treacherous waters since all perspectives are valid. The statement that our plane is a relatively primitive one is a reflection of the failure of the majority of humanity to appreciate our oneness and the self-empowerment that is available to us.

(2) PROBABILITIES:

The whole area of probabilities and probable realities is a fascinating subject that could easily fill several volumes. This is one area that was first introduced in the Seth material, at least from my frame of reference.

It seems obvious to us that those experiences we encounter are valid, and those ignored are not. From a larger perspective, however, all ideas that we choose **not** to actualize are carried out in other dimensions – by aspects of ourselves that we are not conscious of. Especially if we have given an idea much emotion and not followed through on it, it will be carried out by other aspects that we can consider "probable selves[1]".

These are physical versions of ourselves that from their perspective would consider themselves to be the **real** you, and you the probable self. It is simply a manner in which the soul can utilize a greater arena of activity, not limiting itself to one version of actualization.

If we have probable selves, then it is a natural extension to visualize "probable worlds[2]" that would be similar to ours, but that have the opportunity to explore different historical paths that our world has chosen to ignore. We move in and out of probable activities constantly, and actually enter probable worlds without realizing it on an ego level. All mental images are valid, and literally activate dimensions that escape our awareness.

1- "Seth Speaks" by Jane Roberts. Chapter 16, Session 565

2- "The Unknown Reality" by Jane Roberts. Volume 1, Section 1, Session 679

• • •

LESSON (53), DECEMBER 17, 1987

The planning that goes into any long-term project involves a certain logic of desired outcome. The steps taken along the way seem to make sense as you see the way toward your objective. When the objective is unclear, however, you may have a difficult time sorting out preparations or even mental attitude. We are being tricky here, not letting on to the upcoming stages of evolution on your plane that seem relatively obvious to us. The reason being, we will not interfere with your free will. **A vibrational shift is a given,** but how it will be received is left open. The planning for such an event is not easy, since you have no clue as to what this energy will feel like or how it will affect your physical world or mental outlook. We would like to provide you with an analogy here.

111

Imagine a situation where you are on a windswept hilltop walking toward a cabin a few hundred feet away. A tremendous gust of wind takes you by surprise and you momentarily can't catch your breath. You keep walking and fight to keep your balance because of the now incessant gusts. You finally make it into the cabin, feeling relieved and invigorated at the same time. Your resources carried you up the hill, and you never really thought you wouldn't make it. You were worried at times on your way up because you had never experienced such a wind. You can hear the howling outside of the cabin as it turns into a fierce storm.

After it is over, you walk outside and are awed by the relative peace you sense. The birds are chirping as if nothing had happened. Physically, trees are down and some buildings are damaged, but you are somehow more vital for having experienced it all. The people you meet are all talking about the great storm and how they survived, and there is a common goal of cleaning up and moving on. This is a weak analogy at best, and we will give you additional insights into the nature of your coming storm.

● ● ●

LESSON (54), DECEMBER 17, 1987

The point of power exercise as introduced in "The Nature of Personal Reality" - a Seth book, is an excellent approach to the insight and feel for your own energy and your ability to direct it. As you have used it (Michael), it has the potential to offer glimpses of space/time relationships, the connectedness of your greater self, and the connection of your sensed identity to nature. It turned out for you to be much more influential in terms of later events in your life than the natural hypnosis exercise(1) which you felt at the time was the key to manifesting what you desired. To your surprise, you found that simply trusting in your abundance in this case was far more effective than visualizing wealth obsessively – because, of course, you had conflicting beliefs that got in your way. The point of power exercise was much more productive for you

112

because you had no emotional roadblock to deal with and you approached it with little anxiety.

The exercises we are introducing can also be approached with little anxiety because the outcome is detached from your view at this time. We encourage readers to **approach these exercises as a game** and practice with a trust and faith that your newly gained skills will be quite valuable indeed to all of you who are persistent. These exercises work on many levels. You can experience immediate results in the area of mind expanding altered states that will greatly enhance your awareness and belief as to what you are capable of accomplishing psychically – which in turn will act to reinforce your persistence in a circular manner.

(1) POINT OF POWER & NATURAL HYPNOSIS EXERCISES:

Transcribing a few lines of The Point of Power exercise onto a tape recorder, I focused on the exercise for many months and came to understand several concepts in more expansive terms.

Realizing that space and time are indeed one became my first emotional realization. "The point of power is in the present... The present is the point at which flesh and matter meets with my spirit[1]. . .". Since our present is created where matter (in space) meets with our spirit (in time), our physical perspective is a unification of space/time. This may seem obvious, but I found that the relationship between space and time offered the potential for considerable contemplation[2].

Having established the power of the present, the next step in changing one's reality is the utilization of The Natural Hypnosis exercise[3]. This has you focusing on your present moment, imagining in detail what you desire. No conflict exists since your desire and belief become one for this time. This visualization gets you excited and has you match the vibration of your intended situation. It is assumed that once the limiting belief is altered, your reality will begin to change. In my case, I focused on a large sum of money, never really coming to terms with my conflicting beliefs "about" money. That stalemated me. I later came to resolve the issue by simply trusting in my abundance, and accept that my

113

financial needs would always be met. This belief has worked out quite well ever since.

1- "The Nature of Personal Reality" by Jane Roberts, Chapter 15, Session 656

2- I actually played with this concept for several years. The lines quoted here are only an abbreviation of the exercise. Overall, it is intended to have the practitioner recognize that their point of power is "now", not in the past or future. This eliminates the possibility of projecting fears into the present. When this realization is emotionally accepted, the understanding of personal empowerment in the present moment is tremendously enhanced.

3- Ibid, Chapter 16, Session 659

● ● ●

LESSON (55), DECEMBER 17, 1987

The power implied in mental terms can never be overstated, for your mental abilities are far more expansive than you realize - just as the channels to your greater self are. The whole idea is to **clear your beliefs** of the clutter that limits your self-identity or self-image in terms of psychic abilities(1). You are all born with varying degrees of intelligence, and that intelligence cannot be measured by your standard intelligence quotient tests. Regardless of perceived intelligence, ingrown in your personhood is the ability to discover who you are and move into greater and greater realms of awareness to the point where you sense your oneness with your greater selves and your planet. Once this is achieved, moving into a belief that you have the capacity to access the coming vibration becomes easier to accept.

Simply practicing the exercises that we are outlining will help open the channels to the vibration necessary to accomplish manipulation of various degrees on your physical plane. The next exercise we wish to introduce involves developing a feel for an approach to **raising your vibration at will.** Relaxation is your first step, as it is with any meditation exercise. Here we suggest you close your eyes, take a few deep breaths, and picture the darkness behind your eyelids as having the capacity to move outwardly in a spiraling motion in all directions – so as to **enlarge the scope of your inner vision.** The symbol can be most appropriate here. Picture two spheres of energy swirling in a global fashion from the center of your awareness and projecting outwardly. You may feel lightheaded as you proceed, but continue until you feel a larger and larger area of expansion. Here you are accomplishing a vibrational shift by simple suggestion(2).

(1) MORE ON BELIEFS:

Just where to begin the process of working with your beliefs becomes the question often asked. Your **initiation of intent** becomes the first step, with the desire to know yourself in intimate terms. Two techniques can be used very effectively in unravelling your present beliefs surrounding any area of your life:

a) Track your emotions:

When you are feeling an emotional charge, take a moment and step aside to reflect on what thoughts you were entertaining just prior to your emotional reaction. You will arrive at the belief behind the feeling.

b) Track your thoughts:

Pay attention to your stream of consciousness. What you repeatedly tell yourself in mental terms **are** your beliefs.

This becomes a process of gauging your emotions or gauging your thoughts. Either technique will give you an accurate picture of your current status. The next step is to sort out your beliefs and develop a feel for where you are limiting yourself. Then, affirmations can be very effective. If done as a game and done honestly, you will reach a point where you will love yourself for having taken the steps to unravel your defenses – and the process has begun!

(2) EXPANSION OF VIBRATION & CREATING YOUR MENTAL SCREEN:

This technique is very similar to how I've initiated out-of-body experiences during periods of meditation. I have found that raising my eyebrows with my eyes closed greatly facilitates the expansion process. Once in this expanded state, the presence of other realities becomes evident that can then be explored by self-suggestion. After several experiments, this framework can be recalled at will and used to set up our mental screen.

This suggested procedure, then, can be considered the first method of facilitating and **containing the circuits** that we are developing.

• • •

LESSON (56), DECEMBER 18, 1987

Only a few exercises are being introduced here, for the idea is not to burden you with technique but to understand the vibrational shift we speak of. This shift can be compared to a tuning fork and the pitch invoked by exerting various pressure on its surface. A finer vibration implies a less dense atmosphere and a construct where manifestation can take place with far less effort. As you move along the scale of physical realities to nonphysical pre-matter states, you are also sliding into faster and faster vibration.

If you could increase your vibration through mental processes to the point where you move out of the range of your earthbound frequencies, you could hypothetically dematerialize. This is somewhat how you achieve out-of-body states to explore other realities, but here you are simply losing temporary awareness of your bodies. There are many varieties of out-of-body experiences where you can still be aware of your body to a degree, or seem to be at two different places at once.

The reason manifestation becomes easier with a faster vibration is because the connection between thought and end result, **cause and effect,** becomes known as a simultaneous process. Your denser vibration has acted as a **testing ground** for emerging consciousness to explore the power of their thought. This had to be done from a perspective where these connections weren't so obvious, so as to develop an understanding of the affect of their thought and actions on themselves and others. When the connections are known and obvious, a discipline is now needed to "think responsibly".

Once you have reached a level of awareness where you are taking responsibility for your actions and the thoughts that are behind them, you are in a position to experience reality from a vantage point where you immediately see the product of your thoughts. The inhabitants of your planet (en masse) have decided to take a giant evolutionary step with the help of many interested energies "outside" of your plane. We feel a tremendous joy in being a part of your decision, and welcome you into a realm of understanding of infinite love and compassion where you can sense your oneness with the creative process itself.

● ● ●

LESSON (57), DECEMBER 18, 1987

Cause and effect only makes sense from a perspective of physical reality where the vibrational pattern is slow enough to distinguish between cause and effect. In our reality, for instance, there is no distinction – since what we "think" is manifest simultaneously. This is true to a relative degree along the scale of physical to nonphysical planes. We do not mean to imply that cause and effect will have no bearing on your plane after the shift in vibration but do wish to point out that it will be seen as an attribute of your illusion or camouflage.

Part of our intent in giving you a preview of your probable earth changes deals with settling the issue of **pending doom** as forecast by some of your literature. The holocaust implied from a shifting axis is a remote possibility for some – but again, only for those who on some level have a need to experience a trauma of that magnitude. The majority of people will experience disorientation, but a general openness to change and an acknowledgement of intuitive pathways will go a long way here to help assimilate the psychological shock.

The end product, in your terms, will be a **planet of relative enlightenment** where much of the illusion that you so dearly hold as reality is stripped away. At the point where your egos have adjusted to the freedoms these changes imply, you will be freer beings indeed, and compassionate to a degree that will surprise even the most benevolent of your souls. For you will sense the "connectedness" on all levels of existence and between all participants of your plane.

● ● ●

LESSON (58), DECEMBER 19, 1987

The boiling of water changes a substance that is apparent to your physical senses into steam, which still is semiapparent, to a blending in the surrounding air which is even less apparent. None of you would question that process since it can be explained by your physical laws. The manner that this water is now contained in your atmosphere is a good analogy as to **how the coming vibration will be contained** in your environment. You won't see it, but you will most definitely feel it. It will empower your thinking process to a marked degree, and as you experiment with it, you will discover immense potential in your thoughts. It will at first be overwhelming to some, but you will discover that it is not harming you in any manner. You will become more and more comfortable with testing the potential of your new awareness.

To the layman, it will soon become apparent that directed thought now takes on new meaning, for the result of thought now becomes almost immediate in noticeable terms. To the scientist, the power inherent in this process becomes immense as a "source" capable of propelling objects through space in a way that would have seemed ludicrous before the presence of this vibration. To the psychic, the powers of the mind are now quite open to accessing other levels of awareness by simply relaxing and directing thought along lines of intent into greater and greater avenues of unlimited perspective. And to your perception of the flora and fauna, a new vitality that was always there, but with a greater awareness and sensitivity.

You all will appreciate the utter splendor of the godhood expressed in the dandelion, and the aura of the shade tree as it spreads over your veranda – and the shade next to the rock becoming one with the fence next to the barn which becomes one with the cows inside. The animals now seem to be able to talk to you, in a way that you couldn't understand before and nature as a whole has a voice and a power that must now be reckoned with. You won't sense a need to control nature any longer, but to respect its aspects of belonging on an equal footing with even your own. A new deal is struck where there is a mutual and symbiotic understanding of all participants in your grand illusion.

"We are not speaking of a shift in the axis of your physical planet, but rather a shift in vibrational frequency that will carry you into the arena of your divinity with far less effort than you currently imagine."

Chapter Twelve

POWER OF INTENT

LESSON (59), DECEMBER 20, 1987

The **power of intent** is tied in, of course, with the power of thought – but intent carries thought further into the directional process that offers leverage to your already powerful thought. Intent can be said to add density to your thought, not in any negative sense, but in a way that empowers that process no matter what the objective. Intent is **all inclusive** with regard to belief, ideal, expression and direction. There is no room here for clutter and disbelief if approached with a clarity and "innocence of ideal". Innocence here can imply any area of value or perspective and the process can be effective in any direction of ideal.

The concept can be expanded further to incorporate the "circuits of intent" we have spoken of – and there are no limits to the number of participants in any given direction of ideal. These circuits will be explored further for insights of the power contained therein. The process can be approached from many perspectives but the starting point, of course, is always thought. We at this time would like to walk you through the **process of formulating intent.**

• • •

LESSON (60), DECEMBER 21, 1987

Intent can be broken down into components of creation that in total would mimic the creative process of your physical world. Your world, as well as all other worlds, was created through a process of yearning that gained momentum in a simultaneous and spontaneous burst of probabilities in the context of an ever expanding eternal now. You can envision tapping into this primordial energy and newly creating your circuit in the same way as you were created. You are using your most awesome gift, your gift of creation. Your creative abilities utilize your thoughts as the all encompassing spring board that translates abilities from vaster resources outside of your time and space into a format that can be useful for your specified objective. The filtering process itself is accomplished on subconscious levels, but here you can **objectify the process(1).**

Know that the source of your intent is none other than "All That Is", in your terms now, momentarily allowing that portion of itself to flow onto the scaffold of your thought, building up a framework that carries your intent further and further into the circuit of your influence. This circuit can be likened to a **band of energy,** highly charged, for the sole purpose of carrying your thought into a transfiguration of physical response. It is as though your thought, any thought, can take on cosmic importance of first priority if you deem it so. Your next step becomes a visualization process where you are allowing no gap in comprehension so as to **maintain the vacuum of your intent** in an uninterrupted process of completion that simply carries this knowing throughout your sphere of influence back to your original thought.

(1) OBJECTIFYING THE "PROCESS":

Each step in understanding "Continuous Energy" involves the translation of a subjective concept into a useful schematic. Formulating intent is obviously a mental endeavor, yet by breaking down the process into observable procedures it can be "objectified" for purposes of practicality.

● ● ●

LESSON (61), DECEMBER 21, 1987

The knowing of the power behind your thought is an integral part of the process we will further describe. An **empowerment of intent** with the added simultaneous awareness of your connectedness to your godhood carries you over the brink of intensity required for the transfiguration of thought into manifestation, whether it be in general terms or the simultaneous release of energy. **Your atomic structures** in the physical sense are combined in such a way as to **respond to thought** in a conscious manner long forgotten by your cultures.

There is a willingness and a cooperation involved that needs some explanation. The atoms of a given object on your plane combine in a manner responsive to your intent. You individually and en masse emit a psychic energy to form the very objects that your physical senses "then" interpret as reality. The objects, which could more accurately be described as **projections,** are being individually and constantly created with continuous infusions of energy. There are no objects that deteriorate with age as such, but rather a situation where lesser and lesser concentrations of energy are expended into the object of your focus – and where you or no one else is focusing, the object literally does not exist!

Since you are all individually creating your own objects through your own projections, you are agreeing on the placement of these objects in a telepathic arrangement with all else on your plane. To the perspective of an energy not tuned into your vibration or frequency, your world would not take on a physical appearance to the degree of believability or interpretation of your physical senses.

The actual atoms in question that comprise your physical structures have no idea whatever of the manner in which you interpret their union, i.e. a table is comprised of atoms, yet the atoms themselves have no inkling of their tablehood as such. They joyfully combine for your benefit as well as their own **value fulfillment**(1). They (the atoms) are constantly blinking on and off to the dance of their particular vibration and to the vibrational range of this plane. If this process could be slowed down, you would discover that they are actually at their off-cycles and not a part of this reality as often as they are seemingly present. When they are at off-cycles, they are part of other realities and other times. So it is not that your reality is an illusion as such, as much as it simply would not take on a physical appearance to an observer outside of the vibration of your time and space.

Try to picture the **unified field of thought** as awarized units of consciousness ever present at all points of focus. It became the intent of your plane to create a physical illusion and now you collectively desire to change the guidelines of that illusion. You desire to narrow the gap in the process of cause and effect, hence you are acquiescing to a higher vibration to guide you through this process of knowing. **You can access this vibration** as soon as your intent meets with the gestalt of understanding required to carry you over the threshold. If your thoughts are directed in such a way as to enter into a communication pattern with your various atomic structures, they will joyfully respond to your new intent.

The challenge here is to learn how to communicate with your atoms, and this is tied in with the neutron implosion process we spoke of earlier. Your thoughts carry the requisite power to effect this process in a way that can be directed by intent. To maximize your leverage in this regard, we will conceptualize the process via a visualization procedure that will employ a schematic of atomic structure as it responds to thought(2). The concentration and mobility exercises are meant to help implement the energy flow along angles and intensities that will further empower this process.

(1) VALUE FULFILLMENT:

Given the simultaneous nature of time and the open-ended perspective of choice, durability is maintained by value fulfillment. The simplest definition of value fulfillment would be the exploration of endless values[1]. Even though it appears that durability is maintained by seeming physical reality, this perspective is an illusion and the emotional responses and memories we carry with us are the reality.

In earth terms, value fulfillment can be any area of focus we wish to entertain and emotionally enrich, i.e. a relationship, gaining proficiency at a particular sport, concentration on history, art, or any area of interest. From a nonphysical perspective such as the

Orion energies, our belief in physical reality is of itself a broad form of value fulfillment.

In individual terms, value fulfillment wouldn't pertain to a relationship per se, but rather the emotional highs and lows that accompany the "ride". The ride, or the chase that is an aspect of every focus, becomes the enriching quality that adds to the thickness of the value fulfillment. We are conditioned to look for end results - getting the mate, the job, the object, enlightenment, as an end in itself. The actual emotions that accompany the desire and the expression of the chase becomes the essence of the experience that stays with us, not the end result.

Therefore, to envision the taking of a shortcut in reaching a specific goal – or being given an instant solution to a challenge, really does nothing to enhance an appreciation for the experience. There would be a tendency to come up empty handed because that phase of the value fulfillment is short circuited – and hence no appreciation for the chase.

1- "The Coming of Seth" by Jane Roberts. Chapter 10, Session 54

(2) QUESTION: (2-5-90)

What emotional fulfillment does an **inanimate object,** such as a table, enjoy?

A table is not a table from its perspective, but a gestalt formation of units of consciousness that combine for your general intent (en masse) as well as the other realities they are participating in (on your off-cycles). If you deepen your awareness level to yet another facet of expression, these units are combining not only for your benefit, but for the benefit of "All That Is" in its desire to manifest in multiple foci for a most joyful expression of "being". The units themselves cooperate because each is a representation of "All That Is" and recognizes its status as such.

Having no sense of free-will in this regard, it none-the-less rejoices in its awareness of "freedom" in the entertaining of these various expressions. A greater understanding of free-will is required here to appreciate **freedom without free-will.** This is an area that will be addressed in a future manuscript dealing with "The Composite Consciousness of Your Planet - and the Changing Focus of its Intent".

• • •

LESSON (62), DECEMBER 22, 1987

The ❁ symbol given earlier and the suggested mind expanding exercise can be well suited for envisioning the atomic structure you wish to communicate with. We are dealing with scales of comparison that don't necessarily have to make sense to you in spatial terms. As you expand your mental realms, you can **create a framework to contain the entire process.** Visualize a screen(1) that is capable of holding the process through completion. There will be a building of intensity through a simultaneous act of expanding your inner vision ❁ , setting up your screen, visualizing the atomic structure you wish to communicate with and carrying through the manifestation process via a circuit of your intent. How you picture your atomic structure will have some effect on the outcome, so we will describe several alternatives.

If you were to reference an atom from a textbook, it would appear as ⊘ with the electrons spinning around the nucleus. The interesting aspect of this model is that from a spatial perspective, it shouldn't even make sense physically because you are observing mostly "empty space". There is ample "room" here to **step into the vacuum of your atom and encapsulate the neutron** in such a way as to blend with it. Here you will utilize several of the mobility exercises, and in a process that we will label - **estracation,** you will develop a feel for estracating neutrons in an **implosive** manner that you can then direct to complete your circuit.

The energy release that will follow will seem to be mental at first, but will soon reveal itself as having the potential to act in quite a physical manner. We are dealing with **quirks** here that engage folds of energy that "prime" your neutron for purposes of mutual expression. We suggest that you review the lessons given thus far for a feel as to where we are now heading.

(1) CREATING YOUR MENTAL SCREEN:

I first became aware of utilizing a mental screen in Jess Stearn's book, "The Power of Alpha-Thinking". This book impacted my meditation style as I developed the habit of creating a screen as an actual mental workshop in which I would experiment with healing techniques and other forms of visualization. My mental workshop, in that case, was furnished in detail and recalled at will. It is suggested here that a similar screen can be used to contain the estracation process and the circuits that we are developing. (The creation of your mental screen is also mentioned in Lessons 55, 70 and 79.)

"Know that you have been created from this original explosion of being, and that you dwell in the loving thrust of an eternal validity and a most marvelous multidimensional connectedness that you are just beginning to glimpse."

Chapter Thirteen

EGO & EARTH CHANGE

LESSON (63), DECEMBER 23, 1987

The fountain of youth in your literature addresses the ideal of eternity and beauty from a stance of linear time perspective. You have all the time you need, since you are eternal beings – although there comes a point where you have outgrown your myths that once offered some structure to your experience. We are part of the energies that are most interested in opening up your thoughts and awareness to issues that have kept your planet at a stance of relative ignorance for longer than you had planned. Your **ego development** was meant to act as a tool and a means to discover who you are and what you are capable of understanding through directed thought. But you have allowed your egos to over extend their boundaries into areas that weren't meant to be addressed by this portion of your being.

You can conceive of your ego as that portion of your greater self that views physical reality in a reflex manner so as to bridge the gap between your thoughts and the seeming results, or world of appearance. In this way, you can actually realize the outer appearance or status of your reality as a gauging mechanism(1) to recognize the state of your thoughts, i.e. the selection and clarity of the thoughts you are entertaining at any given time.

When in your evolutionary past you had to act fast to procure food or flee from danger, your ego provided a sense of differentiation that at the time wasn't even natural. You saw yourselves as one with your environment, but have allowed your ego to develop to the point where many of you now consider it as the totality of your creaturehood. The time has come to realize that your **egos can be** expanded(2), and can indeed grow along with your increasing awareness and comprehension that you are multidimensional beings of vast potential. It is our intent to rekindle your awareness and acceptance of that potential.

(1) YOUR PERSONAL ENVIRONMENT AS A GAUGING MECHANISM:

It has been stated that "life is a mirror onto itself" and so it is. If we step aside for a moment and reflect on our immediate surroundings – our relationships, state of health, finances etc., it becomes apparent that an inventory of our thoughts and emotions becomes the "creator" of this environment. In other words, our life circumstances at any given time are a perfect reflection of the inner environment of our mental and emotional state. We can observe what each facet of our experience is mirroring back to us, and recognize that if any changes are to be made, they will have to be "inner" changes.

(2) EGO & EARTH CHANGE:

Our egos have been ripped apart by many philosophies and seen as an undesirable aspect of our personhood. Once we realize that it is inseparable from our totality, it can be accepted and convinced to expand along with us. Until this expansion is begun, it is easy to consider it as a much greater part of our focus than it need be.

One facet of earth change becomes the growth and merging of our ego, not the elimination of it. It will still be quite apparent, but will not maintain the same influence on our overall perspective. It is only in this manner that we will be able to appreciate our oneness and connectedness.

• • •

LESSON (64), DECEMBER 24, 1987

Thought-form and intent combine to offer you a semblance of rudimentary understanding of "All That Is" as it embarked upon a simultaneous creation of all realities, physical and otherwise. This creation still continues. Some of the mystery of this creation will make more sense to you when your plane undergoes its vibrational shifts in the coming decades – for along with these shifts will come a better understanding and feel for simultaneous time that now seems so baffling to you(1). With this understanding comes a knowing of thought-form and manifestation as a single process. A new gestalt is then formulated in the aura of your beings and collectively in the aura of your planet that incorporates a vibrational pattern of this knowing.

At this time, your evolutionary path will have taken a major leap as passing energies will now feel welcome to make "their" presence known. This will open an era of cosmic commerce that will indeed expand your horizons of international trade(2). There will be no tariffs in this regard – as an openness to new constructs of thought and accomplishment will feed on themselves and a yearning will begin that will carry you into still another phase of your evolutionary path.

A glimpse of these paths will bring you still closer to your potential as physical beings to express yourselves in infinitely more creative ways that will return you to an awareness that you are not limited in your bodies. You will now have the freedom to divest yourselves of your **camouflage(3)** at will, and for indefinite periods experience reality from an infinity of perspective. It is toward this end that you are directing yourselves as yet another probable earth emerges.

(1) SIMULTANEOUS TIME:

When we are born, we move "into" a time perspective from a less time-orientated environment. Between lives, then, cannot be measured in terms of years or centuries to the personality involved. Value fulfillment contains the arena of experience, not time. There are no origins or beginnings to this construct, but rather a spontaneous manifestation that created the notion of time to come to terms with the potentials implied in the creation itself.

(2) COSMIC COMMERCE:

Within the blueprint of earth consciousness was the intent to utilize our planet as a showcase and model of physical focus and beauty. Resulting from this model was the notion of sharing the products of our consciousness with our galactic neighbors. This was never born out in linear history, but with our vibrational shift comes a renewal of this intent.

(3) CAMOUFLAGE:

Camouflage refers to the "set" of root assumptions made on our physical plane that define the boundaries of our experience, i.e. time and space, cause and effect, and the belief in a physical environment (discussed in Lesson 5). There are an infinity of focuses that can be explored by learning how to divest ourselves of our "camouflage". The most obvious method is the use of various meditation techniques. In this context, the only real separation between our camouflage and another's would be the range of vibration being acknowledged, and this can be expanded with practice.

From a larger perspective, camouflage acts as a protective barrier that keeps us within the bounds of stimuli that we can handle. Therefore, we will only access a vibration and subsequent camouflage that we have the capacity to interpret and integrate to some degree.

• • •

LESSON (65), DECEMBER 25, 1987

The impression you currently hold with regard to physical reality is such that it is a given, whereas your thoughts and feelings about this given are relatively impotent. It is, of course, the other way around and it becomes your challenge to accept this premise in the realm of your understanding and belief. We inhabit a world where there are no physical props as such, but by the same token, we can create them at our discretion for a variety of amusements. The whole point is that your belief is so tied to your physical senses that when you close your eyes, your world should then disappear (seeing is believing)! It doesn't of course(1), but you are playing a similar sort of hide and seek with your beliefs and the very feelings and intuitions that tell you that you are more than your bodies. Your bodies are indeed your most intimate creations, but so is the entire physical field around you.

The boundaries of your perception can expand infinitely both inwardly or outwardly, since all perception is an attribute of thought. You can never get away from thought in any context and hence **the potentials of thought** becomes the focal point of this book. We would like you to develop a feel for the concept that your thoughts, and the emotions they invoke, connect you to all aspects of yourself – and in that same manner, to all aspects of All That Is. As you increase your awareness of these connections you will discover **pathways in your knowing** that will enable you to grasp ever increasing gestalts of who you are and what you are capable of creating by directed thought.

These concepts can be approached from any number of perspectives, and it only takes an understanding of one of these patterns to jiggle your cerebrums into a spark of acceptance to carry these knowings still further. Where you start makes no difference, as long as you have made the commitment to understand that you are capable of knowing who you are to an ever expanding degree. This knowing and commitment will automatically lead you to mental and psychic experiences that will prove to you that you have potentials far beyond the images you hold of yourselves.

(1) SEEING IS BELIEVING:

This comment ". . . when you close your eyes, your world should then disappear", reminded me of a statement found in Lesson 61, ". . . where you or no one else is focusing, the object literally does not exist". Curious as to what "really" is there for us when we close our eyes, I asked for an explanation.

This question has to be approached with an understanding of relative perception and the intent of the experiment itself. If you were trying to prove this theory in a laboratory, it would be very difficult since the apparatus utilized to establish this proof would hinder the results – "the intent here creates the focus". It remains true that where no one is focusing, the object does not exist. Relative perception excludes the nature of the experiment in that you have collectively chosen to view an objectified universe. Therefore, it becomes difficult while embraced in that universe to prove this fact to yourselves. It can be proven, of course, by experimentation with the nature of consciousness – but your institutions do not support this level of proof at this time. From our perspective, it is quite obvious.

Simply closing your eyes does not eliminate the overall focus, but various activities such as sleep do preclude your need for physical perspective. If, hypothetically, everyone on your planet were in a deep sleep at the same time, your planet would not exist in the way that you understand it.

• • •

LESSON (66), DECEMBER 26, 1987

Poker is a game you play for fun or profit where you count on luck or your ability to bluff. Bluffing here is a most interesting sport, since you are at that moment unsure of the outcome, but you continue with the game. Now there is a semblance of approach when we compare poker to the game of visualization where you also have no assurance that your thought pattern will materialize – no more than if your bluff will win you the pot. The point is, you can approach your visualization exercises as a game – not worrying about the outcome at the time, but believing in the process as vividly as you can and trusting that you are engaging in a most useful endeavor.

There has been much literature written in the 1980's on the **power of visualization,** and the revival of this art has been no accident. Visualization incorporates the most basic gift that you have all been given, your ability to create. The leap from visualization to neutron implosion can seem a bit spectacular, but we maintain that if approached from a proper understanding and framework, it is indeed not only possible, but will prove to be quite practical in your coming decades.

The progression of this book has vacillated from concept, to theory, to potential practical application and at times seems to jump around in circular fashion. This has been our intent, for this isn't a text book or a novel, but a book that will hopefully open your eyes and imagination to an acceptance of your vast potential, and an appreciation of how you can channel that potential into a meaningful format within the coming vibrational shifts. **You don't have to wait for these probabilities** to take hold, but can embark on a journey of mind expansion right now. Acting as pioneers in that regard, you can indeed accomplish quite amazing physical feats through mental process. We will continue with our explanation of circuits of intent and the mental requisites involved to wrap up that portion of our book. There will be more books of ours that carry these concepts further – and in that regard, you can consider this work a primer.

"When we speak of a vibrational shift entering your plane, we are suggesting that your holding pattern relative to the desired vibration you wish to contain is being expanded."

"You need no other energy source beyond the mental and psychological power within your very cells that is itching to be unleashed."

Chapter Fourteen

QUIRKS & INVERTED QUIRKS

LESSON (67), DECEMBER 27, 1987

Circuits of intent can be considered as completed thought-form construction where the sender is in control of the process from initiating the act, empowering the intent, estracation of neutron, and flow of subsequent energy release within desired boundaries. This is a mental process that can utilize the conducting rods we will say more about. The mobility of thought exercises here enable the sender to manipulate through various bends and postures to lead up to the peak neutron implosion and estracation process that brings yet another variable into the picture. As the neutron is imploding, the implosion process itself automatically attracts an energy mass at the other end of your coordinate point that can be considered an inverted quirk. You are here **re-arranging antimatter** to allow its entry into your polarity of vibration. This in turn brings vast amounts of fresh perspective and potential into the process.

Your inverted quirk becomes one with the process at the point of peak intensity, and visualization becomes intertwined with process so as to make the distinction unimportant. The process of neutron implosion itself invites inverted quirks into the act by the very nature of coordinate point attribute(1). It becomes an art to distinguish where and to what degree that neutron implosion process carries you, so as to bring these added intensities into your circuit. This perhaps sounds complicated at this juncture, but it will make more sense to you after you have experimented with and reached some success in these realms.

137

(1) QUESTION:

How do you attract a coordinate point in each circuit, and why does each coordinate point lead into realms of antimatter? Aren't there infinite perspectives to be reached by looking into coordinate points?

These are interesting points that will take some time to get into, which we don't wish to do at this juncture. Let us now say that as you indicated to your friend Mark on the telephone this afternoon, your world is being constantly created by an infusion of energy from outside of your space/time, into your psyches, that simultaneously emerges into a projection that you consider physical reality. There really is no point "outside" of your space/time of course, since we are still dealing with thought.

For convenience sake, let us create a model where the "unified field of thought" lends itself to the co-creation of infinite worlds of the imagination. You have collectively decided to create a physical world as a medium to better understand the power of thought, from a cause and effect perspective. Now, this co-creation continues with each physical breath and on levels that are beneath your physical and mental awareness. You are constantly translating thought into physical attribute, and you are doing so via coordinate point activity that helps make your world appear physical in the first place.

In other words, the very nature of your creaturehood incorporates coordinate points as the method of construction that translates units of consciousness into pre-matter thought-form, into physical reality. Now there are seeming stages to this process, although it occurs quite spontaneously. The term **coordinate point**, as we use it, applies to the transfiguration process itself that powers your thoughts that in turn creates your camouflage. There are relative degrees of camouflage, and each one of you controls a coordinate point that is genetically coded to your own personal blueprint that helps you maintain your seeming individuality.

There are greater intensities of energy that genetically contain your planet's coordinate points – and plants, animals, rocks, seas, etc. all have their coordinate points to help maintain the overall thrust of a continuous creation. There are many perspectives that can be applied to coordinate point manipulation and there are no boundaries as such, but **vibrational tones** and **bands of intensity** that separate one level of coordinate point activity from the next. Your creaturehood incorporates coordinate points in overall perspective of creation, as well as in each thought you entertain.

As to the "other side" of these coordinate points reaching realms of antimatter, this is a convenient approach to the discussion since we are dealing with a "matter concentrated system". If you were part of a nonphysical plane, we would be describing coordinate points of varying light and sound values that are not easily translated into the context of this discussion. This becomes a topic for another book if you are so inclined.

● ● ●

LESSON (68), DECEMBER 28, 1987

The **inverted quirk** is more than a theoretical occurrence, for it was a major tool in your ancient historical perspective where these realms were considered quite practical in terms of affecting the quality of their physical reality. They did not hold as firmly to their belief in the five physical senses proving or disproving their scientific theory, and relied much more on intuition to bridge the gap between the obvious and not so obvious. We are speaking of Atlantis, of course, and many of your populace have chosen to reincarnate at this time in your history and probability to be a part of the awakening of these memories.

Atlantis was a series of cultures, collectively settled on a land mass now part of western Europe and the Atlantic Ocean. Part of the geographic area collapsed into the sea after its inhabitants collectively decided to physically end this experiment. At its peak, it was a marvelous demonstration of scientific ability intertwined with intuitive perspective, together which yielded a far reaching understanding of mind/matter connections that are just emerging in your time.

139

The downfall of those cultures was tied in with emotional issues, namely a gap that developed between scientific know-how and emotional growth, as to how to assimilate this knowing into a cohesive package that would incorporate an "evolution of compassion" along with engineering feats. Politics entered into the picture as to who and to what degree the overall population would benefit from this know-how. Large groups of people were subsequently left out – "third-world" you might say. The cellular memories in your own psyches are now reacting as a remembering, to help you to not only re-awaken these abilities, but to insure that you don't make some of the same mistakes again.

• • •

LESSON (69), DECEMBER 29, 1987

Popcorn emerges from seed when heated to break-through temperatures. It inverts itself as a flower blooming in time altered camera sequence. Now, just as your kernel of popcorn gladly shows its "insides" when heated up, your coordinate point will gladly invert for you when you learn to heat up and speed up your vibration through mental processes. There are many analogies here between our kernel of popcorn and our coordinate point that can help you understand the concept in the simplest of terms, yet give you a feel for the process.

A coordinate point is not visible, but its properties allow for energy transformation that make your sight possible. All physical realities require a "source" of energy for the simultaneous and spontaneous creation of camouflage, that is then interpreted as an operational field of a most believable nature. As you are churning out your operational field, you might say, your coordinate points are acting as popcorn makers that invert the kernels of your thought into the "outside" of projection that your egos now translate as the world of appearance.

• • •

140

LESSON (70), DECEMBER 29, 1987

There are many areas we wish to cover and some will have to wait for later books. Our aim in this volume is to offer an overview of coordinate point concept and energy transformation properties that can be most useful on your plane. An understanding of concept is always the first prerequisite. We then suggest a trial and error period with the concentration and mobility exercises. **Each reader will develop a feel for their own mental screen(1)**, and adopt whatever meditation technique they are already comfortable with to our suggested program.

We have been purposely vague in the area of suggested exercises in this first book because we want to first outline the importance of the potential of thought in understanding your world better. Once a level of understanding is reached with regard to how your illusionary operational field is created and sustained, it becomes a major source of **leverage** in the visualization stages that follow. We will give you several additional exercises in the next volume after a framework has been developed to fully appreciate the context of these exercises and the result that can be obtained.

(1) MENTAL SCREENS:

Tips on developing this screen can be found in Lessons 55, 62 and 79. It begins as an exercise in imagination where the screen is created and filled in or outlined in any manner that seems comfortable. After several meditations, it will become easy to recall this screen and use it as your mental workshop that will contain the circuit procedure.

"A vibrational shift is a given, but how it will be received is left open."

"Whether you accept the potential of your creaturehood now or later you will ultimately prove to be a moot point."

Chapter Fifteen

EXTRATERRESTRIALS & THE PYRAMIDS

LESSON (71), DECEMBER 30, 1987

Conducting rods can be utilized to carry out or temporarily "store your intent" along the path of your circuit. Programming these rods involves a process of thought-form projected and stored in a way known to your **Egyptian civilizations** that guarded certain treasures of the great pyramids(1). The material of these rods can be glass-like or crystalline, having properties of an orderly atomized construct similar to your meditation type **crystals** which we will say more about. How the thought-form is stored in the crystal and re-activated takes an understanding of the independent stance a thought takes after it leaves your awareness. The creative process is such that all energy contains awareness(2) to a relative degree, so it becomes a matter of emitting thought-forms of certain peak intensities that you can then work with in this regard. Once you create a thought-form, it cannot be taken back as though it was never entertained.

Your awareness of thought is such that it seems to move in an orderly fashion, although you don't remember what you thought perhaps an hour ago. Larger portions of your being, however, do remember all of your thoughts and categorize them along the lines of emotional intensity. In other words, your subconscious stores all impressions that your conscious mind would have no need or doesn't care to remember. It becomes a process then of bringing to your conscious awareness an art that was practiced in your relatively recent past – of thought-form manipulation and **impregnation**

143

into desired form and focus that will enable you to program your conducting rods. The breakthrough will come when you have experimented with the concentration and mobility exercises to a point where you will have developed a feel for your ability to manipulate and control the thought-form process.

(1) EGYPTIAN CIVILIZATION & THOUGHT-FORMS:

How did the Egyptians guard their treasures utilizing thought-forms, and how successful were they?

Several Egyptian cultures studied thought-form projection and impregnation as a form of voodoo and religious belief to guard their sacred artifacts. Those who gained proficiency at this art were looked upon with great awe and respect for the feared harm they could perpetrate onto others. The use of thought-form in this manner worked to a large degree because the masses believed it. You have to understand the context of the cultural beliefs of the times to appreciate this type of burglar alarm system. Had these cultures been less superstitious, they could have utilized these same principles toward far more creative ends.

(2) MORE ON AWARIZED THOUGHT:

The entire understanding of "continuous energy" relies on the knowing that all energy is awarized and conscious. Since our thought is energy, and all energy is conscious, it then becomes logical to recognize that thoughts can take on an independent stance after they leave our awareness. Our thoughts therefore become amenable to a "directed stance" for our circuits of intent once we become aware of the process.

• • •

LESSON (72), DECEMBER 30, 1987

The intensity of thought required to impregnate a conducting rod is a mental process that can be aided by mechanical device. When you have reached a level of proficiency in understanding and projecting thought-form outline, your next step becomes assimilating this outline with a knowing of your godhood and connectedness. This knowing acts as leverage which enables you to reach the peak vibration necessary to activate the neutron implosion process. This in turn leads to estracation and repolarization of antimatter that further accelerates the thrust of your circuit.

This can all be accomplished and contained through mental processes, but we will introduce a fuse of sorts that can be attached to your ears as **headsets** to help you reach a state of prerequisite relaxation – and further, to regulate the flow of your circuit in such a way as to aid in the visualization process and keep your circuit from wandering. The concentration and mobility exercises will prove to be quite helpful here in giving you a feel for the type of mental manipulation these maneuvers require.

● ● ●

LESSON (73), DECEMBER 31, 1987

Estracation needs some clarification in the context of neutron implosion. You can visualize your neutron as a subatomic particle, or from the perspective of the neutron itself, a universe in comparison. For our purposes, we will describe a neutron as a circular membrane of awarized energy that can be objectified and hence visualized. Picture our membrane as a melon with fibrous stands running through its core, which in turn is composed of a bulk mass or background of a vacuum that contains the fibrous matter in perspective and spatial terms.

Now, when peak intensities are reached in terms of mental control, the fibrous strands **fold into itself** – with the surrounding vacuum causing the estracation of its pressure into the process. This releases a tremendous energy, which in turn leads to the core of your coordinate point which will invert itself if the estracation follow-through is handled at sufficient leverage and intensity. The worlds of antimatter begin to reveal their properties at this juncture, which will **repolarize** at the impact of meeting with an imploding neutron – together which will cause a **chain reaction** that can be brought into your circuit for most remarkable effect in physical terms.

This process cannot be learned overnight, of course, but it can be accomplished if proper understanding and commitment is made. The point of this accomplishment is to give you lead time in dealing with the vibration that will be part of your earth changes. The individuals who gain proficiency at these experiments will literally attract the necessary vibration and in turn will be in a position to teach others – and the process will have begun which leads to self-sufficiency with regard to your energy needs in the interim.

• • •

LESSON (74), JANUARY 1, 1988

The neutron properties as described in the previous lesson are, of course, a gross simplification of the actual process that is behind the multidimensional attribute of the projection you consider a neutron. For purposes of our model, however, it can be visualized this simply since the objective here is the unlocking of the desired chain reaction that powers your circuit – and not an accurate portrayal of physical properties as such.

The **extraterrestrials** described by your friend Sheila(1) were indeed utilizing these principles as they were employed in the construction of **the great pyramids**(2). Here, the tall figures "seen" by Sheila were extraterrestrials that were in charge of the project in a most friendly exchange of interplanetary commerce that was more common in that era. The man pointing his finger toward the pyramid blocks that then "floated into place" was indeed employing a circuit of intent utilizing energy fields native to his planet(3).

The man himself wasn't a physical construction as such, but a sustained model of potential selfhood in earth terms that rearranged his molecular structure long enough to participate in your camouflage system. This colony's entire purpose was to introduce this energy potential to the Egyptian culture at that time – and it was utilized for a time, but in a most limiting way. The experiment wasn't considered a failure, however, because the process is now contained in your cellular memory in such a way that can be re-awakened as your vibrational shift emerges.

(1) COMMENT:

Sheila Dugan and I met at a Seth conference in Austin, Texas in June of 1986. She subsequently helped orchestrate a presentation I made in St. Louis in 1987. The above pyramid information was received by her during a meditation at about that time.

(2) EXTRATERRESTRIAL INFLUENCE ON EARTH:

Can you comment on how this alien culture has made an imprint on our evolutionary path?

Yes, Michael. You yourself were part of this "alien" civilization that migrated to your probable earth in the early days of pre-Egyptian resettlement that was fed by the remnants of your Atlantian cultures. You lived on Atlantis, as mentioned earlier, and as that experiment was ended many of you **relocated onto other physical systems** that later re-entered your earth in projects such as this one. Some were on your plane only temporarily, but others settled more or less permanently as you had. Yours didn't involve a space landing as such, but a shift in "planetary reincarnational pattern".

There have been **periodic extraterrestrial landings and surveilance** of your planet for various reasons and for as long as your concepts of time will carry you. These interchanges will again emerge on conscious knowing levels to help usher in your new age of enhanced vibration, since many of these extraterrestrial cultures come from systems that have engaged in these vibrational shifts long ago in your terms.

(3) ALIENS & CONSTRUCTION OF THE PYRAMIDS:

Beginning with my trip to Egypt in May of 1988 (mentioned in Lesson 18), I have had several extraterrestrial contacts – the sum of which have enabled me to piece together what I believe to be an accurate understanding of how the pyramids were constructed.

I will start with an incident that occurred at the Temple of Karnak in Luxor, Egypt. There is an awesome display of ancient

Egyptian architecture situated there near the remains of ancient Thebes. The temple stretches over many acres, enclosed within the city of Luxor, about 200 miles south of Cairo. It is most impressive with its immense statues of the Pharaohs, massive pillars decorated in endless streams of hieroglyphics, magnificent archways, solemn pathways leading to burial chambers, and obelisks that point to the heavens. During a sound and light show in the blackness of night, spotlights shine over a reflecting pond onto these timeless monuments and a loudspeaker booms out in an English accent with the "official history" of these ruins.

I became drowsy and closed my eyes for a few seconds. Suddenly, I was "translocated" to a seemingly physical location, and as a result, felt momentarily disoriented. Extremely vivid images of various hieroglyphics began floating in front of me, and to my utter surprise, one of them came alive – very alive! It had dark blue fur, unlike any color I'd seen before on an animal. This "being" started communicating with me, but at first I could only stare at the beauty and depth of its colors. There seemed to be a multidimensional knowing to this creature that was most fascinating. It telepathically informed me that when these drawings were made, the people knew how to communicate with them. The purpose of this communication was to impart an awareness of the animal's perception of its part in nature and how it viewed the human in this sharing. This would act as a balancing of the human's ego growth that was already becoming exaggerated.

Standing next to this "animal" was an extraterrestrial – not threatening in any manner, but just standing there. I intuitively knew that if I faced it directly, "something" would happen. Overcoming my anxiety, I stared directly into his eyes. I managed to notice that it had a large head, very large walnut shaped eyes with no apparent pupils – and an overall magnetism that was most compelling, yet gentle. There was a tremendous acceleration as I was immediately swept into its "knowing" and I felt totally helpless as a result. Almost simultaneously, however, there was a blending of our perspectives, and a rather euphoric "high" resulting from his vibration.

"He" asked me if I wanted to go back in time and **witness the creation of the great pyramids.** There was an instant of reflection during which time I knew I could back out of this ordeal, but since I didn't even know where I was at that moment, I thought "what the hell!"

Immediately, there was another tremendous acceleration as I found myself at the site of the large pyramid, about half complete. There were people walking around, but no slaves. Standing next to me was a tall "being" that I suddenly realized was my alien friend. He began explaining to me that the "volunteers" would work with the colony of extraterrestrials that were on the planet. The Egyptians would be in a trance and taught how to utilize "inner sound" to move the large blocks of stone. In a process I didn't understand yet, I witnessed a massive block "floating" through the air all by itself, with the E.T. pointing his long thin finger in a directing manner and the volunteer just standing there. It was an amazing sight that everyone seemed to take for granted.

In another encounter about three months later, I was asked if I wanted to return to the site. This time, I was the volunteer. A disorientation immediately descended onto my perspective, but I was again enraptured in the vibration of my host. It was explained that I would be experiencing a bilocation encounter with the stone that was resting on the ground.

I suddenly found myself out-of-body, merging my consciousness with the stone. I was then directed to a knowing of how to utilize "inner sound" as a catalyst, where I could mesh my vibration with that of the stone. In the merging process, I realized that the stone was now weightless since it was one with my consciousness! I simply "lifted off" in my out-of-body state and followed the path that my host was providing and floated the stone into place. To an unaware observer, this procedure would have surely appeared to be magic.

After the completion of the pyramids, I sensed that the "trance" was lifted as the extraterrestrials departed, and the Egyptians now had no idea of the actual mechanics of construction. Hence, the pyramids were not built by slaves, nor did later pharaohs have anything to do with their creation. These happenings occurred about 8,000 years ago.

Chapter Sixteen

CELLULAR MEMORY

LESSON (75), JANUARY 2, 1988

The impetus to create is inborn in your cells, for the memory contained therein holds awareness of the creative process as it interconnects your current perspective with all other perspectives of manifestation. You consider yourselves as tuned into this time and space, however your cells have no such orientation. They gladly cooperate with the gestalt of your creaturehood, but they have not lost their sense of connectedness to all other systems they have been a part of in linear terms and are still part of in greater terms(1). Your cells don't operate with an ego, and as such, quite easily contain their past, present and future orientation to the spontaneous now. Your orientation as a people is quite purposely more narrowly defined, but you have gone too far you might say, in that definition.

The time has come to open up your awareness, to bridge the gap some between who and what you are – to the quite assured knowing that even your cells enjoy. They are most willing to share this knowing with you if you will learn to open up those channels that will make this communication possible. We will offer you some suggestions in this regard that require an attitude that all parts of you are knowing, but none that is superior to the other. When a mutual understanding is reached, this type of communication will flow almost naturally.

The "feeling tones" are then elicited on either end of this circuit that will symbiotically cooperate in an experience of oneness. This will enhance the process in such a way that you will see that you have never been separated from your cells' knowing, but have cut off that awareness for purposes of a more narrowly defined focus of cause and effect. You can narrow that gap in focus by mere intent and a persistence that will lead you to these understandings in no uncertain terms. The earth changes that will be completed in the next 30-35 years(2) of your time are orchestrating this knowing as part of the vibrational shift, and how you accept these changes in large part can be decided now by your opening up at least intellectually to the understandings contained in these pages.

(1) ACCESSING CELLULAR MEMORY:

Cellular memory involves the overall awareness of past, present and future probabilities that our cells possess, but that our conscious knowing does not entertain. Our cells do not operate with an ego and therefore have a keen understanding of other realities they are participating in.

Biologically, our cells die and are replaced in cycles. As the cellular exchange takes place during life, these memories transfer from the departing cells to the incoming ones in an intricate biological ritual. Throughout the cycles of one lifetime, the pertinent subjective memories of that lifetime are coded within our cells. Upon our transition into nonphysical focus at death, this coded information is carried along with us into the "between life" environment.

As mentioned in the introduction, a death experience in 1964 spontaneously began an orchestration of various encounters with cellular memory. Upon awakening in the recovery room after that accident, I experienced a traumatic and dramatic altered state during which time my whole concept of spatial perspective was turned upside down. It seemed that voices were miles away, but visually were only a feet away. The walls of the room appeared twisted in a bizarre shape, and my head seemed to literally be the size of a huge building. I was being bombarded with stimuli I couldn't translate, and overall was quite terrified. I at first thought that this feeling and perspective was attributable to the drugs I'd been given, but I would spontaneously enter this perspective seemingly without warning many times over the next fifteen years.

I came to the realization in the context of reading the Seth material that I had actually been accessing my cellular memory all along. It was frightening at first because I had no framework of belief to entertain this type of stimuli and extreme disorientation. The experience involves a perception of past, present and future events on the part of my cells all at once which translates into a most eerie sensation of massiveness. The same "massiveness" that earlier frightened me now was exciting because of the euphoria that began to accompany this condition, once I stopped resisting it. I eventually learned how to bring on this state by entertaining certain thought patterns and following them through gateways into other dimensions.

(2) OVERVIEW OF EARTH CHANGE:

Earth change can be approached from many different viewpoints. Let us first consider the need to recognize the trade-off of our current limited focus – for what will be achieved in a global reassessment of priorities and the underlying benefit for the mass consciousness. There will be chaos at times, destruction and death – but this must be seen in the context of our new sense of empowerment, connectedness and divinity. And to those that choose to "die", they will discover that there is no death. New potentials will splash over into all aspects of creaturehood, and the togetherness of this challenge will carry us all into a oneness that will shatter all previous separation and fear.

Also understand that moving into the fourth dimension by man is a universal evolution being shared by all aspects of our planet, and beyond. Our decision to orchestrate this expansion comes at a time when all parallel realities and seemingly distant universes are making a quantum leap into new dimensions. We are all connected and our evolution is not an isolated event. Ours is of particular interest, perhaps, because of the "radical shift" in focus we are entertaining relative to the totality of universal perspective.

The time frame of 30-35 years suggested here must be recognized as the beginning integration of our new perspectives. In terms of contrast, these will be the most dramatic and exciting years of change, but there will be many centuries of further growth to explore the endless possibilities of our enhanced awareness.

● ● ●

LESSON (76), JANUARY 3, 1988

Power tools, as you envision them, utilize electric current to energize their motion. The concept is workable since it employs this current in an orderly fashion that cooperates with your intent. A version of this electric current will also cooperate with your intent in a mental process linked to our circuits. Here, however, **the generating system for this current is "All That Is"**(1) imparting its awareness onto the unified field of thought that you are a part of and that is a part of you. This unified field is all around you and permeates all realities, whether physical or not(2). It becomes a matter of developing a rapport with the very energy that you are utilizing to create your physical bodies. Seen in this context, there is nothing impersonal or out of reach relative to this energy, and it becomes a process of learning how to direct it for your desired ends. It will gladly cooperate with you, because it IS you!

You are not separate from it, although your egos would like to think "you" are independent of this energy. For purposes of implementing our circuits, we are, of course, dealing with your egos - since this is a part of all of you that cannot be negated or pretended away. The idea then becomes one of opening up the channels to your ego and expanding that aspect of your selfhood to blend with the energy we wish to direct.

"Energy cooperating with energy" is literally the mode, although you will envision the process as "awareness" directed energy. It is this awareness that we are directing you toward, and if you have been absorbing what we have said thus far, you are halfway there. After the intellectual understanding and acceptance in terms of belief, the second phase becomes an experimental one where you will play with the concentration and mobility exercises - and in so doing, attract the vibration levels that will carry you into the realms of accomplishment that will in time lead you into a stage of evolution where fossil fuels become the dinosaur of your past.

(1) COMMENT:

"All That Is" as the source of this process can seem rather nebulous, yet once it's experienced, it becomes quite personalized.

(2) THE UNIFIED FIELD OF THOUGHT & THE ETHER:

The "unified field of thought" as being developed in this manuscript reminded me of the "ether"[1] that is continuously referred to in occult literature written at the turn of the century. On January 16, 1990, I asked what the connection might be:

The major distinction in popular understanding of the ether and our unified field of thought, is that our unified field **encompasses all reality** – as a "presence" that you described in your death experience (Lesson 44). The typical understanding of the ether is that it is an invisible medium that "surrounds" and connects all life and all inanimate objects – in some cases actually "providing" the life force to the embodiment in question. The distinction here lies in the understanding that the unified field we speak of is ever present and "contains" the consciousness of a most universal nature – and hence a discussion of probabilities and potentials of the "whole" in each and every embodiment.

1- "The American Heritage Dictionary" defines the ether as . . . "an all-pervading, infinitely elastic, massless medium formerly postulated as the medium of propagation of electromagnetic waves". Einstein did away with the necessity of the ether in his theories of relativity, which are discussed in the Appendices.

• • •

LESSON (77), JANUARY 4, 1988

Nodules of thought, or thought-forms, carry relative degrees of awareness from one area of seeming space to another. The mover of this thought is the intent of the sender, whether sent consciously or not. The idea here is to **make it a conscious process**, and re-acquaint yourself with the potential of this concept. Your earth on a grand scale is a thought-form of gestalt energy that wanted physical expression. On an even grander scale, the physical universe is a thought-form of a still greater gestalt of energies that wanted other experiments in physical expression that would add to the mosaic of potential and probabilities. The energy behind these creations is always conscious and awarized, and as it reaches crossover levels of intensity, its intent becomes manifest. We are speaking here of creation in linear terms for the sake of simplicity.

Because you are all one with this energy, you have been given the gift of creation and thought-form construction. It behooves you to **accept your gift** in a more knowing manner, and so we offer you an instruction manual of sorts. As simple as they appear, the concentration and mobility exercises are gateways to further techniques that will in turn open infinite pathways of creativity. For those who choose not to experiment along these lines, we ask that you attempt to understand these concepts to the best of your abilities. As momentum builds and successes are materialized, even the loudest of your skeptics will start to pay attention and wonder what magic is in the air.

Chapter Seventeen

CONTINUOUS ENERGY, TESLA & EINSTEIN

LESSON (78), JANUARY 5, 1988

A conscious awareness of the **thought-form construction** process becomes our next topic. How you create any thought is a given that you take for granted since it requires no effort on your part. These thoughts seem to come and go as you move through your days. The visualization process (in general) carries this procedure into a more knowing stage since it urges you to pay attention to the formation and direction of the thoughts you are now entertaining. **Our next suggested exercise** becomes a visualization process where you are paying attention to how you are directing your thought, and setting certain "values and boundaries" to your construction. The **values** here refer to intensities and tones that will come alive as you begin to experiment. The **boundaries** become an ever expanding knowing of the reaches of your mind.

You will become aware of various gestalts of thought patterns that will appear and afford you the opportunity of setting boundaries (or) moving on to the next stage of our process. When this becomes second nature, you will have a much better understanding of the circuits of intent we have been speaking of, since our circuits are dealing with consciously created thought-forms that are manipulated within the arbitrary boundaries of our intent. The intensities or values reached will become the gauge that we will utilize to measure the vibrations we are attaining. Gradually, through a combination of intent and thought manipulation, you will discover to your amazement that you will be attracting the awesome power we are hinting at and which you (Michael) confronted in your out-of-body experience leading to this manuscript(1).

(1) PHYSICAL ACTIVITY WHILE OUT-OF-BODY:

Out of curiosity, I asked if one is entertaining an out-of-body perspective, is it possible to alter the molecular structure of a given physical object? If so, is it not possible for mischievous conduct to enter into conscious out-of-body experiments?

It becomes an issue of many questions popping up with each new awareness you glean relative to our process. To address the issue of altering the molecular structure of objects you are focusing on while out-of-body, you don't alter the actual molecular structure of the object that is perceived in physical perspective, but you do indeed alter the molecular structure of the object as it appears to your now expanded senses. The object in your altered state is not molecular in the same manner, however, but you are none-the-less altering its properties – and by an almost simultaneous occurrence, you are then affecting the object in question (that others are perceiving in physical terms).

This is an involved question you are asking, but let us say that the connection between a physical object and the out-of-body appearance of that object, becomes an issue of **relative perception.** We are dealing with as many different "objects" as there are observers because each observer creates their own object whether they are in their body or out. From an out-of-body stance that is close to your physical vibration, your object will appear physical at first glance. But from an out-of-body stance farther away from your home station, you won't sense your physical constructions the same, if at all. There is a difference in molecular structure and concentration of energy in each projection, whether observed from physical perspective or not. There are many variables here as to relative perception, and for the purposes of our circuits and the out-of-body states involved, you will not have to concern yourselves with these levels of perception.

With regard to your question of moving physical objects while out-of-body, it becomes quite possible if an understanding is clarified relative to how that object is being created in the first place. The **ghost** example you just discussed with Mark is possible because of the intensity and circumstances of our friendly ghost in question. You are quite accurate in your conclusion that the ghost doesn't necessarily realize what it is doing in physical terms and in that sense is indeed experiencing a nightmare of sorts. "He" is able to move objects to a degree because of the manner in which he is entering your perspective, which is through intent intermingled with natural abilities that are being subconsciously utilized here. You indeed have the ability to move physical objects from an out-of-body perspective, which we will discuss in subsequent lessons.

As to mischievous behavior resulting from this awareness, we have no comment since free will is always involved. Although to the individual who develops the proficiency required, it would be rather startling to observe this type of intent – for in the process of reaching this proficiency, our hypothetical buffoon would build up an awareness of his godhood and connectedness and not be inclined toward this type of behavior any more than your oversoul playing tricks on your physical stance.

● ● ●

LESSON (79), JANUARY 5, 1988

As you were just discussing with your friend Mark, **thought within thought** and the simultaneous streams of consciousness that can be directed or held, are indeed key concepts of our circuits of intent. You are capable of maintaining several layers of thought at any given time – and you do in fact hold numerous layers beneath your conscious awareness all the time! We are referring to simultaneous reincarnational existences and probable systems that may or may not be physical.

The **amount of thought** that you hold at any given time can be consciously increased to contain many more such streams or currents. In your concentration exercises, you (Michael) came to the conclusion just the other day (refer to Lesson 24) that you could visualize your apple from many different perspectives and still hold the image, i.e. behind a glass window, on your ashtray, flying through the air, etc. These are areas that will be explored in greater detail after the basics are introduced and mastered to a workable degree. We are still dealing with thought-form construction and will continue along those lines.

When you create a thought-form on conscious levels, it will be helpful to first isolate your thought and frame it into the shape of your intent. We are being arbitrary here, since there is no beginning or ending to a thought, and isolation of thought is not possible. But for our purposes, we will set parameters for the sake of understanding. Framing your thought(1) will be our first step and we suggest visualizing a frame in your mind. Within this frame, create a picture of an atom with an electron (one electron for simplicity sake) spinning around the nucleus. It is spinning very fast, but through a process of slowing down its vibration, you are entering into the area of the nucleus.

Now, picture your neutron as a large round sphere that has membranous strands permeating through and around its outer surface, keeping in mind that it is a vacuum that holds this sphere together. Merely develop a feel for this process as carried thus far – and after repeated exercises, you will find that you have created a thought-form that can be recalled at will. In other words, re-creating your neutron will become easier and easier because you are re-attracting the same thought-form you erected earlier. You are not literally attracting the same thought, but a replica that has been stored in your cellular memory. We are ignoring the electron and proton because they have no bearing to our circuit at this time(2).

(1) FRAMING YOUR THOUGHT:
Framing your thought as described here can be considered part of the earlier suggested procedures for creating your mental screen (Lessons 55, 62 and 70).

(2) QUESTION:

Why is it necessary to visualize the entire atom in the beginning of this exercise when we are simply dealing with the neutron?

The visualization process we suggest incorporates the entire atom so as to lend itself more believable at this stage and make sense to you. We are re-introducing concepts that have long been forgotten by your cultures and bridging some gaps in your understanding of matter as it relates to thought. In so doing, we must work within the framework of your beliefs. It is not absolutely necessary to visualize the process of slipping into your thought-form, but you will discover that it becomes practical in developing a feel for the next exercise we will introduce.

QUESTION:

Does jumping into the thought-form of our projected atom involve an out-of-body experience of sorts that will allow added control in the manipulation of our circuit?

Yes, Michael. Our process is now making sense to you in an accelerated manner. As you gain proficiency at framing your thought-form and then blending with it, you will have an out-of-body experience of sorts where you will **bilocate** and not lose stature of your physical stance – and at the same time, be quite able to direct your circuit since **you are now one with its energy**[1]. From this perspective, you are able to blend with the object of your intent for a most remarkable result.

1- COMMENT: (11-1-89)

The answers to this and the previous question resulted in a remarkably similar description of how I experienced the pyramids being built (mentioned in Lesson 74). The timing of these events was of interest to me because my extraterrestrial encounters were four months to a year after this lesson was drafted. It is becoming clearer and clearer to me that I am experiencing sporadic altered states, that in total, are providing me with a rounded exploration of the requisite tools needed for an understanding of the "process".

LESSON (80), JANUARY 6, 1988

Practice makes perfect is the old saying, which has relevance here. You don't need to be perfect, of course, but at least comfortable with the process as outlined. You will discover your own feel for each stage which will make each succeeding maneuver a logical progression. The **tones** for each layer of thought you are able to entertain will all have their own individual feel and vibration. This will benefit you in your ability to distinguish them, and **direct specific strands** at your discretion.

The out-of-body, or bilocation phase, occurs after you have maintained a balance between your strands, have their tones in perspective, and have reached sufficient levels of intensity to interact with our neutron. This interaction will involve only one of your strands, which you will then blend with for purposes of following through within your circuit. The remaining strand will remain in place and act as director, keeping track of your home station, as well as the movement and accomplishment of your circuit's activities and movement.

The prerequisite to these abilities of bilocation involves a balancing of awareness along two lines, and our **concentration exercise** is geared toward this end. The **mobility exercises** will help you develop a comfortable feel for following through on the activity of our circuit. The headsets we mentioned earlier will be utilized once these stages have been developed, and our crystalline conducting rods will fall into place after individual successes are recorded in sufficient numbers to consider group activity.

The time frame for bringing these activities to fruition depends on each of you, but from our perspective we can see it in the realm of probability as occurring within the next 6-7 years of your time. Successes can be achieved very quickly(1), but we are speaking of enough experimentation to develop a cohesive front for the implementation of group activity that will show you initial results in terms of your energy needs. Here, of course, there won't be a complete self-generating front, but rather a series of individual accomplishments that will encourage others to join in the challenge (in geographical pockets) and in that manner spread throughout your continents.

(1) TIME FRAME FOR INITIAL RESULTS: (11-1-89)

What is the time frame for the success of initial results and what is my role in this regard?

The probabilities of occurrence are changing as your time passes. There has been a tremendous "opening" made with regard to new age thought as a result of several well-known personalities making their beliefs known. This trend is evidenced of course by the proliferation of channeling, the many workshops, and simply the number of new age books reaching your marketplace. To answer your questions leaves some room for error, but we see initial demonstrations of a successful nature approximately **two years** after publication of this manuscript.

Your role, Michael, is to help market the book by personal talks, workshops, etc. You have several additional books to write in this series but you will still be able to teach and/or demonstrate several of the techniques leading up to the circuits of intent we speak of. The extent of your success in these realms will depend on the commitment and time allotted for coordinating your efforts in an uninterrupted time span that you will allow for such experimentation.

You are accurate in your assessment of the last lesson – that you have indeed experimented with the majority of "altered states" needed to get an overall feel for the process outlined. This does not mean that the onus is on you to prove the point. There will be many others jumping on the bandwagon to take this role.

● ● ●

LESSON (81), JANUARY 7, 1988

Developing a feel for these strands of consciousness will be your next step as you discover them in your concentration exercise. They don't have to be discovered in this manner, since you entertain different layers of thought each time you daydream or are half listening to an uninteresting conversation. We will focus on our concentration exercise because it serves many other purposes as well. The exercise will come easier for some because many people are naturally visual in their imagination process, whereas others are more feeling. You all have the capacity to obtain satisfactory results, however, if you are persistent. As you are looking at your apple, it will help to imagine that you still see it even though your eyes are closed. This imagining helps you to not only keep your image intact, but also to open up your "inner senses" that will be utilized for the remainder of your circuit's activities.

The beginning stages of this discernment requires only a feel for these layers. As you get more and more comfortable with entertaining two strands of thought, your next step becomes one of gradually **projecting one of your strands** to various imagined physical locations in your room. You will be immediately capable of directing this strand to farther reaches, but the problem becomes one of losing sight of your other strand and defeating the purpose of our experiment. So frame these processes in the room you are practicing in and before you even begin, give yourself a suggestion that you will remain focused on your apple regardless of any intruding thoughts that may enter your awareness during this time.

A timer here becomes helpful to help you keep track of greater and greater periods of concentration ability. It is not necessary to go beyond 15 minutes. When you consistently reach the point where you can hold your image comfortably for this period, alternate between this and several of the mobility exercises (in every other day fashion) until you have experimented with all of the images we have given you.

• • •

LESSON (82), JANUARY 8, 1988

The **progression of steps** will move as fast as you set up your expectation and persistency. It requires no particular awareness of the mechanics involved, but more a knowing and trusting that you are capable of achieving proficiency. Success feeds on success, and as confidence is built up you will feel inclined to share your experiences with others – and the proliferation of an understanding of "continuous energy" will have begun on your plane. It will be helpful in the beginning to establish a schedule as to when you will practice and, of course, stick to it as much as possible. **Other aspects of your greater self will be alerted**(1) to your intent and will joyfully offer their assistance in helping you move along. A chain of events occurs where many observers are waiting anxiously to share in your growth, and as each barrier is lifted, we feel as joyful as you since this is a multidimensional joint effort.

You won't recognize your old self in the coming decades and will marvel at the growth that is possible while still in physical perspective. You don't have to wait until your planet undergoes its changes and this becomes an important point. The more of you that open up to these overall levels of awareness the faster your planet is healed, hence necessitating a lesser shift in what you would consider unsettling terms.

(1) UNSEEN SUPPORT & MAKING A START:

The urgency of healing the planet in a timely manner "guarantees" an unlimited level of support by each readers guides, extraterrestrial brothers, angelic realms, aspects of soul, etc. Understand that the support you seek **and** the level of response (to earth change) you will be capable of integrating, will be in direct proportion to the degree you know yourselves and recognize your soul connection. THE BENEFITS ARE UNLIMITED! Consider a smoother transition into the 4th dimension and the payoff it offers you **now** in terms of your overall well-being and sense of empowerment.

Since God or "All That Is" is within us, it becomes a matter of **knowing ourselves** to the point of witnessing this divinity within. This can only be accomplished by looking inwardly and addressing the beliefs and emotional issues that tell us we are unworthy or limited. This is a process that has been evolving for eons of our time and one that becomes a major thrust of earth change.

It becomes important to **open up** and connect with your own energies and your own "issues". Open up your heart and allow your energy to be focused through that aspect of self that trusts in its own becoming. Vibrational shifts are stimulating that openness. Learn to develop the trust that there is nothing within you to fear. WALK INTO YOUR FEARS and allow yourself to look into your personal issues. Metaphysical knowing and understanding earth change does little good if it's not integrated on an emotional level.

In overall terms, you begin to grow by **facing** the situation, the person, the opportunity – with a direct and heart-centered response. Open up to the levels of communication you've been blocking, and start with your own inner dialogue. You must begin with where you are now. If you don't acknowledge your current status, you can't change it – because you can't release an emotional pattern that you don't admit to owning. By not admitting to current fears, you are in effect keeping yourself in a status quo situation.

For those "serious seekers" out there, here's a technique that has helped me. In private, you can actually begin to "invite" your fears into your focus, embrace them, and say, "I love you fear!" And **feel that fear** build up in your stomach, and move into your heart chakra and be transcended into personal empowerment! It works! Understand that your fear energy is the same as your love energy, but with judgement placed upon it. If you're looking for a challenge, this process will **automatically** attract the support you seek.

• • •

LESSON (83), JANUARY 9, 1988

Passing through geographical territory on your physical plane is analogous to passing through layers of thought, although the senses you utilize to measure "distance" in the latter are not physical. Developing an intuitive feel for the layers of awareness that you are capable of holding begins a process of expanding your identity to include latent aspects of mind that have been dormant for eons of your time. Once these levels are discovered and observed, it becomes a matter of practice that leads up to the intensity and projection necessary for our circuits. The first step is to simply **develop a feel for the presence of these different levels,** and hence the subject for our next exercise.

We suggest that you play with this awareness as you are waking up in the morning after several hours of sleep, but before you have opened up your eyes. This period of your day is one of your most relaxed, unless of course, you have had an unsettling dream. Suggest to yourself before retiring for the night that you will wake up very relaxed, and before opening your eyes in the morning you will become aware of your ability to entertain two layers of thought. Your ability to wake up without opening your eyes may prove elusive at first – and you can attend to this exercise during any other period of meditation during the day, but this awakening time may require the least effort.

Now, at the point you are awake and relaxed and with your eyes still closed, focus on your normal stream of awareness for a few seconds. Then project a thought that will move "around" this first current and notice how you are quite capable of maintaining a hold on both. You may experience success on your first attempt or it might take you a few weeks of repeated attempts to get a glimpse of this potential. After you've had a few successes in this **elemental bilocation,** it may be practical to attempt this during the day and add this to your other mobility exercises given earlier.

QUESTION:

I was told by two "psychic" acquaintances this afternoon that several well-known historical personalities including Albert Einstein are involved in the production of this book. Is this accurate?

Yes, Michael. They are all involved, as well as numerous other personalities on the sidelines who are not directly involved, but are none-the-less most interested in the evolution of the principles set forth in this book. Einstein[1] in particular is concerned with the development of a nonpolluting source of energy to replace the atomic dinosaurs present throughout your globe. It is not Einstein the man that is concerned, but the soul energy of that personality as it now has blended with your intent and focus. Einstein is dead in your terms, but his world view **and** current perspective are both involved in your work on a very close scale and concern. Between the many of us that are involved for our own reasons, you have a rather credible bandstand of support to work with and call on at your pleasure. Your curiosity in any area that will further explain and unravel these concepts into a cohesive, workable package will be especially welcomed.

1- ALBERT EINSTEIN & NIKOLA TESLA:

The influences of Albert Einstein and Nikola Tesla have shaped the scientific evolution of the 20th century. In 1905, Einstein gave the world his famous equation $E=MC^2$, which equated energy and mass. This became the bedrock of understanding that led to the splitting the atom in 1932, the theoretical creation of an atomic bomb in 1939 and the dropping of that bomb in 1945. With the advent of peaceful fission and nuclear energy, several variables sprang up that Einstein didn't bargain for - the potential for nuclear accidents and the mounting problem of how to dispose of nuclear waste.

Nikola Tesla's alternating current motor began the electrical revolution around the turn of the century. Considering the scope of Tesla's contributions and the fact that he has been all but forgotten, led me to the undertaking of drafting a summary that would tie together the legacies of Einstein and Tesla, with a cosmology incorporating the input of "Continuous Energy". This attempted "synthesis" can be found in the Appendices.

● ● ●

LESSON (84), JANUARY 10, 1988

After becoming comfortable with your ability to maintain two strands of consciousness, it now becomes a matter of learning how to blend the second with objects along its path and effect desired change. This will require a knowing and feel for various energy levels and **discerning entry points** into each. If you imagine a layer of steam dissipating into the air, it finds its own path by seemingly blending with and disappearing as it becomes less and less observable. You will find your own path in a similar manner, by visualizing your essence surrounding the object in question and becoming one with it. As you observe its vibration and **personality(1)**, your blending will become an automatic by-product of your intent and you will continue with your maneuver, taking "you" and the "object" with you.

The process, in other words, becomes one of **symbiotic symmetry(2)** between you and the object. You are not even aware of being separate at this point – and you will initiate the process of estracation and reformation of antimatter to further empower your circuit into the next stage. This process can be repeated as often as necessary, with your "home station current" discerning the direction and completion of your intent. Those observing this process will only "see" you concentrating on these maneuvers, but these sometimes doubting observers will have unmistakable proof in the reading of their instruments and/or the mobility and energy release associated with them.

The process will be repeated in various locations and before various audiences until enough publicity has been generated to attract funding from private means as well as governmental agencies to move the application into a stage of practical use in scientific terms. You (Michael) will be the initial spokesperson until others are able to mimic your understanding and process.

Your friends Pat and Gloria(3) were quite accurate in their input at your coffee break yesterday – and knowing that your man Einstein is involved in this manuscript should not intimidate you at this time. You and Einstein are both coming from a most mutual and loving perspective in terms of shared ideals and your "meeting" was orchestrated by this concentrated overlap of intent. Pat's analogy of the dandelion blowing seed throughout your lands was a clear image of the travel your book will imply. You will indeed be led to the right place at the right time, and meet with those who will be in a position to carry on with our joint efforts.

(1) PERSONALITY & ENTRY POINTS OF ENERGY TONES:

These are subjective concepts that can only be discerned by practice. Just as repeated dream symbols can take on their own personality, so can meditation symbols.

(2) SYMBIOTIC SYMMETRY:

This phrase impressed me as being awkward at first, but it does offer an awareness of the blending that is achieved by merging with the object in question. From my own experiences in merging my consciousness with other life forms, it did become obvious that there was a definite cooperation involved with the object of the merging.

(3) COMMENT:

Pat Ross and Gloria Kopac are mutual friends of mine. Pat has been involved in metaphysical circles for many years and simply closed her eyes for a few seconds and got the image of the dandelion. Gloria tuned into the "Einstein connection".

• • •

LESSON (85), JANUARY 11, 1988

The outline as supplied thus far gives you a glimpse of the process as it will be implemented in practical terms. Only a succession of emotional and experiential demonstrations of repeated successes will prove to your (Michael) questioning mind the practicality of visualization as a tool. You don't give yourself enough credit for how far you've come in the last few years utilizing visualization as a framework for change. Here, visualization is being suggested as a framework for far reaching and further change involving your physical world as it appears to your senses.

You are creating your world in the first place through a visualization of sorts, along with the energy of "All That Is" as it visualizes a universe of probable manifestations. The very thrust of your being implies terms of cosmic relevance and interaction with the very energy you will learn to direct. **You can never separate yourselves from this energy,** (but) only become more and more knowing of your connectedness to it. The problem here is that the word itself has been overused in unspecified terms and has lost its credibility to those who have tried visualization seemingly without success. The key, of course, is the combination of visualization coupled with an emotional realization of belief and intent that yields result.

Here, we are implying a format that is incorporating the knowing that you are divine beings capable of changing the rules of the game that you yourselves have set up. Whether you accept the potential of your creaturehood now or later will ultimately prove to be a moot point. The view of your physical world as an unyielding given and your psychological state as the variable must be unstructured. For the two are inseparable and the power implied in this knowing is the energy source we speak of. You need no other energy source beyond the mental and psychological power within your very cells that is itching to be unleashed – and show you what can be accomplished through your conscious direction.

"Advancing these theories into practical application terms won't be as esoteric or unwieldy a process as you fear."

Chapter Eighteen

FORMATTING YOUR INTENT

LESSON (86), JANUARY 12, 1988

Formatting your intent becomes a process of deciding what your objectives are in any given circuit. Carefully considering your maneuvers here is a key process to the successful manipulation of energy folds for your best leverage and result. After several practice circuits, you will develop an individual feel for the most effective **primer visualization** and subsequent carry-through for each situation. You will discover that different motions will be better suited for different tasks.

For example, if your objective is to create energy release to be utilized for **powering a vehicle,** you would concentrate on initial intensities to break through the necessary barriers of estracation that would in turn be directed to your hypothetical drive train. This technique will propel your vehicle over land, or with a simple modification, through the air. It then becomes practical to store your initial thrust so as not to overpower portions of your ride while underpowering other portions. Here, crystals can be utilized as a carburetor of sorts that will monitor the consumption of your thought as it is released in an efficient manner. Many of the **spacecraft** that periodically visit your plane utilize an energy source of this nature, although their technology(1) has moved beyond these initial understandings.

If your objective is instead one of **manifesting** a given item, you would again prime your visualization. But for this maneuver, you will utilize a process of outlining your desired object in mental terms and then filling it in with the release of your circuits' thrust. You are here creating a pre-matter construction that will emerge into your reality as a child filling in a coloring book. You are the artist, and you become the creator. The object doesn't necessarily materialize before your eyes, but it does enter into your experience under the guise of ordinary events and circumstances.

If your intent is to generate power for your **heating needs**, you now prime your visualization for an energy release into your generators that in turn will act as a typical coal or gas power plant you now utilize. The potentials here are endless, therefore consider this an overview of possibilities. Your initial experiments will be utilized for demonstrating the moving of objects in measurable terms. The exact breakthrough of these maneuvers is left open, but know that the end result will be a series of manipulations that will prove most useful in assimilating the vibrational shift you can look forward to.

(1) MISSING TIME:

A classic encounter with "missing time" on September 11, 1988 developed into a firsthand appreciation of spacecraft technology. I was returning from a trip to Winter Park, Colorado where I had been speaking at the 5th Annual Rocky Mountain Seth Conference. The airplane ride from Denver to Chicago had been normal enough, but United Airlines flight 629 from Chicago to Milwaukee turned out to be more of a ride than I had expected.

As I was leaving the conference I was greeted to a grand farewell that seemed rather strange at the time. As I boarded the elevator, and before the door closed, Barbara Marciniak (Lesson 18) began frantically waiving good-bye. The commotion brought a dozen or so people out to the lobby to see what was going on. They in turn began waiving good-bye which attracted still more people. The farewell lasted about five minutes, which left me somewhat baffled.

By the time I arrived in Chicago, I was tired and somewhat irritated by a few events that had bothered me during the conference. There was an outlandishly dressed man in front of me on the escalator which had me chuckling, as I proceeded to board that airplane in a rather blase mood. The first thing I noticed was that there was a woman sitting in my assigned seat, which irritated me further since that plane was almost empty. She was occupying my window seat, so I calmly sat down on the aisle seat, mumbling under my breath "the nerve of that woman". She was dressed rather strangely in an ensemble that blended very well, despite the fact that she seemed to be wearing clothes from several different centuries. I didn't speak to her, and we only made eye contact once as I was staring at her bizarre garb.

There was a delay as I patiently waited for what seemed to be a half hour. As I was reading a magazine, this woman next to me abruptly bolted out of her seat and mumbled some incoherent comments about being on the "wrong craft". She darted over my sprawled out feet, proceeded a few yards up the aisle, and dematerialized! She was there one second and gone the next. I didn't know what to make of it. Assuming I had imagined that event, I continued reading my magazine. I got more impatient because the plane wasn't moving, and for some reason, never took my correct seat. What appeared to be twenty or so minutes later, the same lady re-appeared and excused herself as she took my seat again. I noticed that she looked 45-50, but had a timeless look about her. She promptly fastened her seat belt as the pilot simultaneously announced that we were landing. I was totally confused, since we had never taken off!

Either I was getting spacier than normal, or something very strange indeed had occurred. It had been on my mind the entire next day. Sheila Dugan (Lesson 74) called me at work that day and talked about her and her daughter Kate's recent "alien sitings" during Sheila's meditations and Kate's dreams. She asked if I had ever been "abducted". I had to think about that and responded that I hadn't (at least consciously). On the way home from work, I played a channeled audio tape in my car that talked about "being who and what you are". When I got home, I was uneasy about my job as a stock broker, feeling that I could quit at any time but not sure how. I felt very empowered while listening to that tape and promptly asked my guides, via automatic writing, what had occurred on that airplane ride the previous day and how did I miss the takeoff?

ANSWER:

In physical perspective, the airplane did take off, but your consciousness missed the event. You left that plane to bear witness to the probable earth you are going to witness in mass terms. You joined us for instructional purposes of a pre-arranged orchestration of events dealing with your role in this regard. You have in fact visited us in our mutual "plane of learning" where we have interacted many times before. This is not a dream landscape, but a locale that you have the option of visiting at your conscious will - if you allow it. For now, simply recognize that your confusion yesterday symbolized a move into new probabilities for you in which you will pursue your books and workshops full time. (I did quit my job October 27, 1989 and have been pursuing a "metaphysical" career ever since)

QUESTION:

How did I get home from Chicago?

You got home on the airplane in a sense, but simply were removed in a gentle way for your "class" and your symbolic change of probabilities to take place.

QUESTION:

Was this an abduction?

Not quite. It was different in that it was not a physical abduction you are used to reading about, but an agreed upon abduction in which you voluntarily met us half way.

Suddenly, I had an awareness of the strange lady on the airplane who bolted out of "my" seat, mumbling that she was on the wrong craft. I spontaneously remembered the "craft" I found myself on! Awed by the beautiful lights that were built into the round walls, I stood there fascinated by the rich shades of blue and peach that blinked on and off to a code that somehow enabled the merging of our vibrations. There were short beings walking around in an insect-like manner and the same taller being I had met in

Egypt four months earlier. Instead of taking me back to the construction sight of the pyramids, this time was spent explaining my role in terms of earth change. I also recalled a simplified explanation of how to verbally channel their energies. For the time being, it was suggested that I project my ego up and to the right side of my head, and allow the words to flow up the left side of my vocal cords.

a) "Intend" their presence
b) "Move my ego" out of the way
c) "Allow" their thoughts to be spoken

Following this remembering, there was a moment of reflection, at which time I recited an affirmation given to me by Barbara Marciniak . . . "I intend to become a clear channel now!" I meant it and felt that I had nothing to lose and would repeat this affirmation until it happened. I followed the suggestions given to me on the craft, and at first imagined I was channeling until it felt that I was indeed expressing someone else's thoughts. The message was something to the effect that I would channel these beings as an augmentation to my talks. I was told I would be a spokesperson in merging their thoughts on a mutually clear basis that will enhance my role as a speaker. The suggestion was given to end the transmission and digest these happenings.

On January 28, 1990, I underwent a hypnotic regression under the direction of Rodger Berg, a clinical hypnotherapist and friend, with the intention of remembering more of my abduction experience. A summary transcript of that session (with Rodger's induction and comments removed) can be found in the introduction.

● ● ●

LESSON (87), JANUARY 13, 1988

Deciding on a format for your given chore will require some pre-planning in initial stages – although once experienced, this will become second nature. The planning involves sizing up the perspective and the object you wish to interact with(1) and lining

177

up the focus of your thrust. It becomes an extended modification of your concentration exercise where you sized up your apple, i.e. paying attention to physical attributes and how they fit into your scene. Here, you are simply expanding your scene to include the physical space that will be involved in your circuit. You will choose which items you will **focus** on to **blend** with, **pause** at, **estracate** out of, and eventually return to your home station.

There is much flexibility here, and the entire process only takes a few seconds once you have reached the stage of your mental maneuvers necessary to begin. Depending on the objective of your demonstration, you may contain your circuit in the room in which you find yourself, or literally take it around the world and back. As long as you have an idea of what you are attempting, you can set up the **initial priming** to accomplish that end. In your early experiments, we will suggest that you keep your circuit framed in the room of your experiment simply to build up confidence in an orderly fashion. Haphazard ventures here could take you into areas that would not be in the interests of "fair play". We will explain the potential of these maneuvers as we move along.

The remainder of this manuscript will deal with bringing you up to a level of understanding in terms that we have outlined conceptually. We will provide you with enough material to begin your experimentation and follow up with further background and support in subsequent books. We are most anxious to monitor the reaction to this work and will support anybody in the same manner who reaches levels of interest and commitment to carry out these potentials. Your greater selves will do the same, of course, and we are here only reminding you that you are not alone. As you demonstrate your sincerity, you will find these maneuvers much easier than they first appear.

(1) SUITABLE OBJECTS TO INTERACT WITH:

On March 6, 1990, I asked if there were any suggestions as to what objects would lend themselves to these interactions?

The selection of your object matters little in potential terms, but a smaller object may prove more effective in practical terms.

Selecting a piece of wood may prove to be satisfactory such as a smoking pipe, a pencil, a wooden spoon, etc. Your apple would do just as well, or any piece of fruit for that matter. Whatever object you choose, "play" with it and develop a relationship with it. You will sense the capacity to interact with it after a short while.

● ● ●

LESSON (88), JANUARY 14, 1988

Background support for this joint effort will become unmistakable when enough individuals take part in attempts to follow through on these maneuvers. It can be seen individually as soon as levels of understanding and earnest application have been achieved. This is the only way to begin. The concepts as outlined may appear strange only because of the manner in which you, as a people, have developed your beliefs along the lines of cause and effect and physical reality being the **rock bed reality(1)** of your universe. When it is learned that your world literally changes as your view of it changes, you will discover infinite potential to maneuver within that rock bed construct and watch it bend with your intent.

If you look around your physical landscape, it doesn't appear that things have radically changed in your recent past. If you project this same scene thirty years into your future, you assume that it will be essentially the same. Now whether this proves to be the case will depend on how well you adapt to the earth changes that you yourselves have unknowingly set up. These changes, once again, will be of a vibrational nature, with all aspects of your world responding in their own way. Until you have an experiential understanding of what a vibrational shift entails, it is difficult to appreciate what we are talking about. For those who have experimented with different forms of meditation, you can relate these altered states to shifts in vibrational awareness. For those who find these concepts new, just think of how you feel at different times during the day when your world might appear different to you.

179

When you first awaken after several hours of sleep, lying in bed for awhile before rising, it's easy to sense the relative calm of this higher vibration(2). If you feel yourself getting rather excited about anything during your day, this again represents a shift in vibration. If you take a few deep breaths and relax at different times, this represents yet another vibrational pattern of your thoughts. The idea here is to have you understand that you change your vibrational pattern 24 hours a day, quite naturally during different levels of sleep and quite unknowingly during your day as your mood changes. We are now moving this awareness to conscious levels where you will make it a step by step awarized process and frame your vibration into the context of your objective. This will involve an infinitely more effective utilization of the energy that you have always been a part of, but not consciously aware of directing in this manner.

(1) ROCKBED REALITY:

This simply refers to the assumptions we make relative to the parameters of our beliefs and experience. We so firmly believe in our physical focus, that it becomes absurd to think that it's an illusion, and that our "true" reality is one of our emotions and thoughts.

(2) QUESTION:

Is it a "higher" vibration we experience upon awakening from a deep sleep? If so, would this contradict our current thinking in terms of "slower" brain wave patterns during sleep? Or are we talking about two different concepts, "vibration" not being connected to brain wave pattern?

When you first awaken from a sound sleep, you are still experiencing the finer vibrations of your dream journeys. This represents a "higher" or faster vibration from our perspective. In terms of brain wave cycles, your technicians are measuring electrical emanations of the brain that appear to move slower during sleep. Where we differ is in our discussion of higher vibration and your understanding of slower cycles of electric impulse that seemingly occur at the same time. Two realities are in effect merging here as your consciousness returns to your body.

While your consciousness was out-of-body during your sleep state, it was experiencing a faster vibration. Your instruments, on the other hand, are measuring your brain activity which is still connected to your physical body. These become two different measurements then, as you are not measuring vibration which is nonphysical, but brain wave activity which is closer to physical expression. We will further clarify these differing measurements in subsequent discussions of subtle vibrational tones and subvalues of designated manipulations of energy folds. This seeming confusion will also be rectified with an understanding of how realms of antimatter affect your coordinate point activity in the constant creation[1] of your physical perspective.

1- ANTIMATTER & CONSTANT CREATION:

On March 22, 1988, I asked if the physical understanding of "vibration" is related to the imploding and exploding of energy fields that are attuned to our physical senses?

Yes, Michael. There indeed is a link between the nature of vibration and the **imploding and exploding** energy fields that we have spoken of. It is this thrust of energy that is co-created and a by-product of the vibration process itself that creates the physical appearance of your energy fields. It is your physical senses that pick up this vibration for translation into seeming appearance, but it is equally the imploding and exploding "process" that structures the vibration which in turn creates the framework for the possibility of your physical senses in the first place. There is no beginning as to what comes first . . . the chicken or the egg. The vibration of all realities are part of the continuous creation of parallel worlds. Once understood, this will offer significant insights into the "mechanics of creation".

The challenge becomes one of mimicking the mental process as it intersects with vibrational pull. The general understanding of the nature of "vibration" and the give and take of surrounding energy fields will then lend itself to an unlimited scope of practical applications.

QUESTION: (2-19-90)

How does antimatter balance our focus of matter?

An appreciation for the mutual influence of matter and anti-matter in the continuous thrust of creation becomes necessary for the understanding of all physical universes. In a basic sense they are projections, but equally, an environment that is maintained by the balancing of matter and antimatter. To the perspective of a world composed of antimatter, your world would be the one of opposite polarization. Relative perception becomes the key to unravel how each contributes to the other. They actually keep the polarities in balance, not only with each other, but within the constant creation itself. You could not have a matter concentrated system without a balanced antimatter creation of similar perspective[1].

1- During a group meditation at a recent conference I attended, I encountered an experience that intuitively felt like I was slipping into a world of antimatter. The major difference appeared to be one of social interaction, which impressed me as being somewhat altered, but similar enough to be a counterpart of our own. My thoughts seemed to come at a different "angle", in a way most difficult to describe. Physical laws were similar, but some of them reversed. Gravity and electromagnetic properties were evident, but different assumptions applied. Also apparent was the seeming variety of colors and shades of colors that were unlike anything I'd seen before.

• • •

LESSON (89), JANUARY 15, 1988

Vibrational patterns that we speak of are analogous to differing brain waves that your scientists refer to. It is a weak analogy, however, since the range of frequencies possible in even a small a spectrum of your unified field of thought goes far beyond those found in physical expression, and hence in your brain wave analogy. Cycles per second of brain wave activity, or sound emitted from your electronic music boxes, does give you a rough approximation of vibrational flexibility – and that analogy can be envisioned as waves of thought moving through the air.

Let us consider your plane as a holding pattern for a given range of vibration where faster or slower frequencies will blend in. For most experience and physical sustenance, however, only a relatively small range is required. All aspects of your physical world then vibrate within a certain range – and the vibration of any given object or life form in fact creates the illusion of the parameter of that object for your physical senses to then define as solid.

Your mind isn't physical in the same manner, however, and here you have infinitely more flexibility to alter the vibrational pattern of your awareness. Hence you are quite capable of propelling your consciousness out of your physical field altogether, and do just that every time you fall asleep. A major point here is that while your brain patterns do indeed adjust to the vibrational field of your particular plane, your mind has no such orientation. Your brain can be considered the physical counterpart to your mind, but your mind has an equally valid nonphysical counterpart that exhibits the potential to access "any" system throughout the complexities of the cosmos.

Now, when we speak of a vibrational shift entering your plane, we are suggesting that your holding pattern relative to the desired vibration you wish to contain is being expanded. This will allow your senses the opportunity to expand their awareness of a larger perspective of the creative process, and hence a clearer understanding of your connectedness and divinity.

"When we say that you are divine beings of light and love, you can take that literally."

Chapter Nineteen

WHAT CONSTITUTES REALITY?

LESSON (90), JANUARY 16, 1988

In considering the evolutionary path your planet has taken in recent historical perspective, it appears to you that your sciences and psychologies are quite advanced relative to cultures of your past. What is not taken into consideration is the simultaneous nature of time, of course, since that would create havoc in your theories and reveal embarrassing ignorance in your histories. The point is not to start thinking in simultaneous time terms, but to understand that your cellular memory and awareness of the concepts we are introducing are quite currently contained in "their" knowing, and not so advanced or distant to "your" knowing. Advancing these theories into practical application terms won't be as esoteric or unwieldy a process as you fear. Memories of these skills will come to the surface as soon as you open up to the possibility of a self-generating energy source utilizing the very energy of your thoughts.

The main block in this leap of concept into result lies in your belief that physical reality is an unyielding panorama of appearance. When you understand that you are creating that appearance with mental energy and sustaining it with mental energy, it is not so hard to believe that you can alter it with the same energy.

The models of power plants and mentally propelled vehicles that we have suggested are quite literally that simple to operate once a breakthrough is made in learning how to manipulate within, and direct various folds of energy. Estracation of neutron becomes a "visualization of practicality" as your planet undergoes a rather rapid depletion of natural resources that is occurring in your current century. As hypothetical as these processes now sound, they will be a part of your everyday technology by the early 21st century. There will be a transition and technological breakthrough in the understanding of the power of thought and the sacredness of "all" components of your world. This is all implied in your vibrational shift and some of the very reasons for it.

• • •

LESSON (91), JANUARY 17, 1988

Knowing that your world is an illusion to those outside of your vibrational pattern doesn't help you directly in the potential manipulation of your world. It does go a way in explaining how your plane is maintained by subconscious thrusts of energy, through your coordinate points(1), into a projection that you call reality. What we wish to unravel here is **"just what constitutes reality?"** To most people, it is the very projections of their psyches that is the definition of their reality. This is the belief that needs expanding, for your reality maintains its appearance **only** to those who wish to participate in it. Because not enough of you understand these concepts, and have developed at a donkey slow rate in linear terms, you have jointly orchestrated a change in the very rules of the game – in the form of an enhanced vibrational momentum to carry you into these knowings whether you feel ready or not.

Whether these changes will appear positive or negative becomes a matter of perspective. Knowing that you yourselves have agreed to this leap in comprehension can help you to accept these changes and flow with them. To those who approach their sudden awareness in this manner, they will create an infinitely more satisfying experience for themselves. To those who fight these changes, they will be setting up various degrees of inner struggle and seeming hardship. The end result, however, will be a world that is ripe for self-understanding and cooperation that you all ideally are striving for now in fantasy terms. From our perspective, it is a very exciting time and we will make our presence and support increasingly known as your plane moves into these happenings.

(1) COORDINATE POINTS & CONSTANT CREATION:

(8-18-88) This line implies that we utilize coordinate points every moment of our linear time in the very maintenance of our illusion. Therefore, my previous assumption that coordinate points are only found in scattered locations on the planet is erroneous, especially considering the illusionary aspects of space. Is this accurate?

Yes Michael, the manner in which we are using the term here implies the very **process of maintaining your illusion.** This is not to contradict your understanding that there are relatively stronger and weaker coordinate point activities on your planet, but only to point out that the process itself is essential to the very physics of thought-form construction and simultaneous creation of your physical plane. This is true of every physical reality, for even though the physical attributes of your plane are a projection to an "outsider", it is quite real to you – and hence the intent of the coordinate point utilization here is the manner in which your reality is created and sustained. Relative to the introduction of the concept of coordinate points in the Seth material, the statement that there are major and minor coordinate points should not confuse you. We only wish to add, that to various degrees, coordinate points are used in the entire process of physical creation.

Your conclusion that simultaneous time and the continuous creation of your plane (utilizing coordinate points) are tied together, was accurate indeed – for there could be no other way of maintaining simultaneous time without a continuous creation (or vice versa). This is a parallel understanding that can lead to many new avenues of exploration.

● ● ●

LESSON (92), JANUARY 18, 1988

Minor points of our model can be included in this volume or in subsequent works that we will jointly orchestrate. Several unsettled issues such as the programming of your crystals for group activity and secondary stages in the implementation of these energies will be addressed in the logic of importance as needed. The headset for helping to achieve a relaxed state and carry you into higher vibrational peaks will be given to you after studying elementary electronics and physics that we now suggest you undertake.

You have been receiving these concepts to fit into your (Michael) understanding of thought formation and illusion, not your awareness of current scientific thinking on issues of atomic structure and electrical circuitry. This has been quite advantageous thus far, so as not to disrupt our flow of thought by a questioning ego along these lines. The book is finished for purposes of initial understandings. We again toast to our joint effort and remind you that there will be many more such books, limited only by your imagination and curiosity. We love you – and that applies to all who choose to open up these pages.

• • •

Postscript

The ending caught me by surprise. As the book began, it ended in an aura of mystery as to the future of the concepts introduced and what my role might be in that regard. I apologize if the wording of various concepts is confusing. Please understand that these ideas are as new to me in many cases as to the reader. At the expense of diluting the clarity, many of the sentence structures turned out to be relatively long and perhaps unwieldy. As in my approach to the Seth material, I suspect that it will take several readings to appreciate the expansion of consciousness offered in the manuscript, and a belief in the potentials implied.

"The world was not created nor
is it maintained by logic."

"True science would entail an
investigation into consciousness
& the inner universes of the
mind."

Appendix A

AN OVERVIEW OF CURRENT SCIENTIFIC THINKING

Let us begin with the understanding that our entire focus of the physical universe is derived from certain assumptions that we have taken for granted. These assumptions, in turn, have led us into a search for origins and limits – where there are none. In the simplest of terms, our world is a projection created from a perspective outside of time where there are no beginnings and there are no boundaries. What may not appear believable, namely that our physical world is an illusion, is a statement that will gain more and more acceptance as we move through the decade of the 1990's.

Through our overuse of logic, as opposed to a natural balance of logic and intuition, we shall soon recognize the inescapable conclusion that the physical universe isn't solid and that our logic will not provide the "origins" we have been looking for. Acknowledging the creativity and accomplishments of science, it has none-the-less skewed our line of questioning along the path of many false assumptions. Time and space do not exist as we experience it outside the parameters of our vibration. In these terms, physical reality is an illusion in that it is not as we "see" it to those consciousnesses of a different vibrational perspective. A tree and a dog do not view our world as we do, and neither would an extra-terrestrial peeking into our planet.

Consciousness creates the universes of form. There was no "big bang" of gasses and particles that mechanically created our intricate and complex world. And there is no such thing as inanimate or dead objects, since all of reality is composed of the consciousness of original creation. Creation still continues, and within this understanding, time is eternal, simultaneous and forever new. Ours is indeed a free will universe in which our thoughts create our reality. Physical perspective is ever changing dependent on our particular focus at any given time. An appreciation for the potential balance of our intuition and logic is the only way we can come to the knowing that we live in an orderly universe where what we think and believe creates our experience. The belief that the physical universe is a given, while our thoughts and feelings have no bearing on that given, will be unstructured.

It's the scientific approach itself that's being addressed here, and what follows is an overview of how we have come to view the universe in scientific terms.

• • •

Sir Isaac Newton (1642-1727) can be considered the symbology of our current scientific attitude. Although the necessity for "objective proof" had already been set in motion by the mid 1600's, Newton embodies the scientific thought process and methodology that has endured.

Setting the standards for the scientific method, . . ."I make no hypothesis – validity can only be established by the ability to reproduce experiments and come up with the same results." This approach resulted in an unquestioning attitude with regard to the need for "proof" in our overall thinking. "Objectivity" now set the stage for a mechanical universe that could be dissected to see what makes it tick. Each individual event could now be defined by deterministic laws which philosophically removed the value of intuition, and took away our free will.

Best known for his laws of motion and gravity, Newton is widely quoted . . . "If an object is moving in a straight line, it will continue moving in a straight line forever unless acted upon by another force, i.e. gravity"... "Every action is accompanied by an equal and opposite reaction"(1)...

It became understood that the same force that pulls an apple down from a tree also keeps the planets in orbit around the sun. Newton didn't offer an explanation for gravity as Einstein did, nor did his mechanics deal with electricity or magnetism well. Yet our space program still uses his understanding of gravity in determining relative orbits for the accuracy required in rocketry and satellites. In his study of optics, Newton understood light as being composed of minute particles, corpuscular in nature and freely mobile in a sea of the ether(2).

By 1900 there were two competing theories that would describe the mechanics of the universe. Newton offering one and **James Clerk Maxwell (1831-1879)** the other. Maxwell envisioned space as it surrounds charged bodies, like ripples on a pond. He and **Michael Farady (1791-1867)** were originators of the idea of the "electromagnetic field", a so-called basic element of reality that could be broken down no further. Maxwell's equations carried out these concepts mathematically in the 1860's, embodying a field theory of electricity and magnetism. All space was still occupied by the ether, but was capable of being electrically polarized(3).

After delivering a series of lectures in the U.S. and Europe between 1891 and 1893, **Nikola Tesla (1856-1943)** quickly became one of the worlds most publicized scientists. Throughout the decade, his name and achievements were constantly in the headlines as he lectured and dazzled his audiences with his showmanship quality of explaining the nature of electricity. Exhibiting his ingenious rotating magnetic field, it would be utilized in the the first successfully demonstrated A/C motor and it's subsequent use in lighting the world. In quick succession, he was granted 41 patents along these lines, yet few people are aware of this mans genius.

Tesla operated on the premise that everything in nature vibrated, and that earth's vibration corresponded to his alternating current. He experimented with electrical vibrations in all frequencies in an attempt to understand the entire range of vibration that revealed itself in the universe. He built oscillators and endlessly experimented with electrical/mechanical vibrations at differing frequencies.

Demonstrating such marvels as his electric vacuum lamps that required no wires and no apparent "source" of electricity, he continued to amaze his public. A loop around the ceiling of his lab was always energized as one method of lighting his lab. If anyone wished a light at any location, they simply carried a glass tube that illuminated the surrounding area.

Thomas Edison (1847-1931), whom history has credited with being the king of electricity, was working exclusively with direct current. A sensational battle ensued between these two factions, Edison unsuccessfully attempting to demonstrate the danger and unworkability of Tesla's model of alternating current. Tesla's standard version of 60cps A/C current has endured, yet he has been written out the text books.

During his famous Colorado experiments in 1899-1900, Tesla claimed to have observed "stationary waves". This led him to conclude that the planet acted like a "conductor of limited dimensions" – which would allow the transmission of an unlimited amount of power to any desired location without loss. This evolved into an interlocking system of A/C and D/C current, apparently leading toward the development of a particle beam accelerator. John O'Neill, his science writer friend, speculated in the first biography of Tesla ("Prodigal Genius – The Life of Nikola Tesla") that the particle in question would have had to have been a neutron!

Aside from harnessing our current system of alternating current, another of his enduring legacies are his "Tesla coils" – transformers that raise and lower the voltage of varying high frequency currents. In one form or another, this breakthrough is still utilized in every radio and television set(4).

The scope of Tesla's research is astounding relative to how it has collectively influenced our current electronic era. The basic concepts of radio technology were initiated by Tesla as he applied for patents back in 1897, and the timing of who demonstrated the radio first leads toward Tesla before Marconi.

He played with the basics of radar forty years before the onset of World War II, and either patented or discovered the foundations of . . . the automobile speedometer, cryogenic engineering (the underground transmission of electric power), loud speakers and telephone amplifiers, medical diathermy (deep-heat therapy utilizing high frequency current), and various forms of lighting. Tesla's pioneering efforts led to the breakthrough in the development of X-rays, neon lights, guided weapons and radio controlled robots, the transistor and computer circuitry. This is a partial list, and the man remains relatively unknown.

In 1911, he developed a powerful rotary engine that could utilize any number of fuels, develop 110 h.p. with discs 9.75 inches in diameter and a thickness of two inches. He was so far ahead of his time that he began to lose credibility, and totally disagreeing with Einstein's theories further alienated him. "He would not reveal the nature of his discoveries until he had secured patents, and he would not apply for patents until he had made actual working models, and he could not make the working models because he had no money(5)."

Believing that E=MC^2 had no validity, Tesla consistently refused to accept that energy could be derived from matter. For his own reasons, the curvature of space was impossible and removing the need for the ether would prove to be the end of relativity. According to Tesla's version, the ether was a force field that actually energized the physical universe. There was no energy in matter other than that received by the ether, which acted as the invisible medium that light propagated through.

Throughout the second half of his life, Tesla's focus was one of developing a wireless system of transmitting energy. It appears that his views on how to accomplish this changed over the years, but his general approach was one of mimicking the earth's vibration with his coils and thereby setting the earth into electrical oscillation. With simple apparatus similar to a radio receiving set, he claimed that this energy could be tapped anywhere on the planet.

Tesla claims to have perfected the system during his Colorado experiments of 1899. Unfortunately, he failed to develop this idea commercially and we subsequently don't know how close he actually came to a working model.

Also around 1900, the birth of "quantum theory" was established by the work of **Max Planck (1858-1947)**. He noted that some types of light radiation didn't correspond to Maxwell's wave theories. Experimentation with energy radiation and absorption led him to the discovery that excited atomic oscillators emitted and absorbed energy only in measurable amounts, or "quanta". Because of previous experimentation and beliefs in the ether, radiated energy was thought to be wave-like. Energy was not only emitted in quanta, but it was radiated in discontinuous spurts (not continuously). In the process of his experimentation, Planck arrived at what came to be known as "Planck's constant" – a formula used to calculate the "size" of the energy quanta emitted by varying light frequencies.

This notion of quantifying energy was actually initiated by **Sir Isaac Newton**. Planck's discoveries, however, marked the beginning of the "modern" search for the ultimate building blocks of the universe as well as the development of current understanding of subatomic phenomena. Planck's constant, that designated a measurement of "action", was used by **Einstein** in his work with the properties of light and by **Niels Bohr** in his model of the electron. It was also utilized by **Louis De Broglie** in calculating the wavelength of his wave-particles, and as a central element in **Werner Heisenberg's** "uncertainty principle".

1905 saw the heralding of **Albert Einstein's (1879-1955)** Special Theory of Relativity and $E=MC^2$, bringing us the realization that energy and mass are equivalent. The smallest fragment of matter contains a tremendous amount of potential energy and the total amount of energy in the universe doesn't change – but continuously converts back and forth from energy to mass and mass to energy.

There can be no object being absolutely at rest, since there is no point in the universe that can be considered a stationary reference point. Motion and the lack of motion is now totally relative to another object (or the observer). Special Relativity dealt with steady motion and high speed – every motion had to be considered only a "relative" motion. The only statement one could make with regard to the speed or location of two points in space would be their encounters.

It had already been determined that the speed of light "C" is constant and has no bearing on the velocity of the observer. It is always the same, 186,000 miles per second. Einstein elaborated by explaining that in order to measure the speed of light it becomes necessary to utilize a ruler and a clock. The measuring instruments themselves will give different results at different velocities and frames of reference. Clocks move slower and measuring rods become shorter at speeds closer to that of light. Space and time are not separate events, but a continuum of "space-time".

Einstein's 1905 paper on the quantum nature of light won him a Nobel prize in 1921. Back in 1803, **Thomas Young** (1773-1829) had demonstrated that light could be proven to be wave-like. Now, Einstein showed that it also had particle-like characteristics. This initiated the wave-particle controversy that has never really been resolved.

The General Theory of Relativity was introduced by Einstein in 1915, dealing with the effects of gravity on space-time. Einstein postulated that gravity distorts space and time creating "tracks" through space. Light travels along these tracks in a curvilinear trajectory as it approaches the gravitational field of a massive object such as a star or galaxy of stars. Empty space loses its meaning and the need for the ether is "officially" eliminated. Not only does gravity curve space, but it slows down time. If you could hypothetically travel at the speed of light, you would not experience time or space, since distance is also diminished by relative speed.

Einstein concluded that since energy and mass are equivalent, matter is simply "frozen" energy. It is only because of this slowing down effect and the impossibility of achieving the speed of light, does the scope of a physical universe make sense. Physical objects are not "in" space, but are "spatially extended". In other words, space cannot exist independently from the notion of what fills space, and if objects could exceed the speed of light, they would theoretically experience a reversal in time.

An outgrowth of his theories suggest that an intense gravitational field creates the existence of black holes, a region in tracked space where nothing can escape, not even light. This "hole" engulfs all surrounding space and matter. They are believed to be collapsed stars folding onto themselves, creating an intensely massive event with an equally intense gravitational influence. Since light can not escape, time stands still at the periphery of a black hole. Hence, if time can hypothetically stand still, it must be viewed as relative.

Niels Bohr (1885-1962) won a Nobel prize in 1922 for his work in developing a new model of the atom. The electrons surrounding an atom now revolved around the nucleus in "shells" that are specific distances from the nucleus. The electron remains in the shell that is closest to the nucleus, considered the ground state, until energy is added to it – causing it to jump to a further out shell. When the energy is released, it jumps back to the ground state, emitting energy equal to the energy initially absorbed plus light and photons. There is no way of determining which shell the electron will utilize in either direction(6).

Bohr was one of the major contributors to the development of quantum theory. In 1924, he suggested that light was composed of "probability waves", that are mathematical descriptions which can accurately predict the probability of certain events within an experiment. He coined the term "complementarity" in an attempt to explain the wave-particle duality of light, but fell short of a real breakthrough. One of his major contributions was the conclusion that the very act of observing an event alters our observation and our result. What we observe was no longer "external reality", but our interaction with the event.

Louis De Broglie (1892-1987) added a new dimension to the wave-particle paradox in 1924 by suggesting that the electron, an obvious particle, had wave-like attributes – while waves had particle-like attributes. This explained how particles had the capacity to appear where only waves could seemingly penetrate. He won a Nobel prize in 1929 for this discovery and a merging appeared to be in order tying together Planck's "quanta" and the wave-particle qualities of light as proven by Young and Einstein. De Broglie's equations, measuring the wavelength of his "particle-waves", revealed that the greater the velocity, the shorter the wave-length.

The next big jump in the evolution of quantum theory belonged to **Werner Heisenberg** (1901-1976) for his "uncertainty principle". Around 1925, he observed that in subatomic realms it was impossible to ascertain both the position and momentum of a particle at the same time. The more you knew about the position, the less you knew about the velocity and vice versa. Therefore, quantum theory evolved into a statistical evaluation of probabilities. Particles now had "tendencies" to appear, expressed mathematically. He concluded that since it was impossible to really know what was going on within subatomic perspective, science should cease the need to erect atomic prototypes. "All that we legitimately can work with is what we can observe directly(7)".

Heisenberg won a Nobel prize in 1933 for his utilization of matrices, or mathematical tables, that are used in quantum mechanics to determine the probabilities of subatomic tendencies. It didn't matter what happened between point A and point B, but only what tendencies actualized and with what accuracy of prediction. This was a radical departure from previous atomic models that relied on the belief that particles moved in prescribed and observable pathways. Now what was of interest was the statistical probability for the occurrence of certain energy states and the transitions of those states occurring within the observation.

Shortly after Heisenberg formulated his matrix mechanics, **Erwin Schrodinger** (1887-1961) discovered in 1926 that his wave mechanics were mathematically equivalent. Schrodinger had theorized that electrons weren't necessarily particles as such, but "standing waves" that could be quantified. It wasn't sure what was standing, and if you will read back a few pages, it was noted that Nikola Tesla had observed standing waves back in 1899.

Schrodinger developed his theories on the premise of De Broglie's matter-waves, and furthered the evolution of the wave theory of particles. Although Schrodinger's equations aren't compatible with Einstein's theories of relativity and don't work well with "higher energies", they became the foundation of quantum wave mechanics. As a wave function, he described all the possibilities in "isolation" that can occur between point A and point B of an experiment. The attempt is made to measure how waves and particles are altered by external influences.

The challenge became one of measuring and predicting the endless probabilities of atomic events that would actualize under given conditions – all under the assumption of "uncertainty". No one knows why the specific event at point B will actualize, but dependent on the choice of experiments, it could now be determined whether the outcome will be a particle or wave. The mechanics of the process itself and what causes a specific event to actualize is somehow now up to "chance"(8).

Heisenberg's 1933 Nobel prize was shared with **Paul Dirac** (1902-1984) who attempted to apply Einstein's relativity to quantum mechanics. He described the electron in terms of wave functions and concluded that there had to be states of negative energy, i.e. the positron, a short lived positively charged electron was discovered in 1932 – and the antiproton was unraveled in 1955.

Dirac recognized that the smallest of subatomic particles continually changed form. This constant creation and annihilation of particles at the subatomic level led to the belief of individual fields continually interacting with one another. At that time there was thought to be a separate field associated with each particle, which has since expanded to over 100 particles and an equal number of fields! His theories successfully predicted many "new" particles.

Meanwhile, Einstein spent much of his later years attempting to devise a "unified field theory" that would unite the mathematical relationships of gravity(9), electromagnetism, and the nuclear forces(10). The Special and General Theories of Relativity didn't remove the dualism of particle and field, so this became his next logical step. He desired a theory that would unite all fields and be consistent within all observable phenomena.

In his own words, Einstein pursued a theory that would "exhaustively describe physical reality, including four dimensional space, by a field". This unification was never accomplished, noting that . . ."the present-day generation of physicists is inclined to answer this question in the negative(11)". There was his insistence that one must begin with a unified whole, not "quanta". Responding to Niels Bohr's belief in "uncertainty", Einstein once replied that "God wouldn't play dice with the universe".

The understanding that Einstein developed in his equation of mass and energy led to the awesome potential of mass at rest, or energy waiting to be released. This, of course, developed into the splitting of the atom, nuclear fission, atomic and hydrogen bombs, and the nuclear power industry we are now contending with. What wasn't resolved was whether we live in a finite universe or an expanding one.

A most interesting observation is that three of the scientists responsible for the development of quantum theory vigorously denied and questioned the conclusions drawn from their respective contributions! Max Planck, the founder of the notion of "quanta", took no part in furthering the evolution of quantum mechanics. He disagreed with Heisenberg, Dirac and Schrodinger as to the conclusions being drawn by his own research.

Erwin Schrodinger, as it turned out, also frequently spoke out on his philosophical objections to the generally accepted versions of quantum theory – even though his wave functions became the basis for measuring subatomic phenomena. And, despite growing evidence that probability factors had to be built into every measurement of subatomic phenomena, Albert Einstein vehemently disagreed with the "chance" aspects of quantum theory. He argued that the new theories didn't explain reality, but only probabilities of group behavior. This contradicted his cosmic intuition and need for universal order.

Einstein presented thought experiments in the 1930's showing that the position of subatomic particles could be determined. Niels

Bohr, however, responded that these experiments contradicted Einstein's own conclusions of General Relativity. To Bohr, "uncertainty" itself was a requirement for any accurate model of the universe. To Werner Heisenberg, it was impossible to determine the location of any one subatomic particle. The measurements themselves changed the results of the experiments. Einstein could not alter the direction that science was taking toward the belief in uncertainty and chaos in subatomic realms.

• • •

Quantum mechanics itself can be described as the study and behavior of "quanta" within the artificial boundaries of a given territory. The purpose is not to describe what will happen between points A and B of the experiment, but only to predict with accuracy the varying possible transitions and results of what is being observed. It has been determined that every subatomic event is evidenced by the annihilation of the initial particle and the creation of entirely new ones. It is a mathematical determination based on experiments accomplished in "isolation". True isolation is not possible, but the game is played anyway.

Mathematical consistency becomes the ideal of "truth", since it can be repeated in different circumstances time and time again. Mathematics as a language, however, necessarily utilizes the symbols within its own parameters. It cannot transcend the barrier of consciousness or experience, and becomes a trap in terms of its credibility as the "final say". Not meaning to take away from the brilliant mathematicians who arrived at the conclusions already established in the realms of quantum theory, there are limitations to the task of describing the universe in these terms. The range of intuitive knowing that can provide the answers to the mysteries of the universe are unfortunately outside the realm of legitimate science.

The old approach to physics assumes that there is an "exterior" world to observe. Quantum physics has concluded that you can't measure the object of any experiment without changing it, yet most of science ignores this realization. What "old physics" and "quantum theory" have in common, however, is that the same aspect of objectivity is utilized. Old physics starts with the assumption that the universe can be dissected to see what makes it tick, and new physics has the same hang-up in terms of its incessant need to measure the quanta.

In the process of quantifying energy, it came to be understood that particles consistently reconstruct their form. What was formerly thought of as "mass" continually creates, annihilates and re-creates itself again. Particles collide, transmute and blink in and out of existence. All particles, in fact, have a potential existence as different combinations of particles, i.e. protons momentarily change into electrons, neutrons, etc. Every particle now has its antimatter counterpart, and the meeting of two similarly charged particles automatically causes the destruction of both(12). This dance lends itself to the belief in chaos beneath an outer appearance of order – a logical conclusion without an understanding of simultaneous time and the underlying "units of consciousness".

And, to spite the "accurate" conclusions of quantum theory, the parade continues to find the ultimate building blocks of the universe. This search is grossly misdirected since it's already clear that mass and energy are equivalent and subsequently convertible one into the other. Therefore, finding any particle will unleash its wave counterpart and no conclusion possible.

Funding is continuously sought for larger particle accelerators that have the capacity to project quanta at higher and higher speeds for purposes of observation and proof of ever smaller particles. At the time of this writing, the U.S. has asked Japan to share in the now estimated $8 billion cost for the worlds largest supercollider. By going bigger and faster, it is hoped that this super lab will further define the structure of the atom and finally determine the formation of the universe. When an understanding of constant creation is acknowledged, the realization will be made that the current approach is analogous to chasing a paper dragon.

All of science is a random approach in that each component thrives on its own independent specialty, ignoring most others. The result has been incompatibility and competition between the different disciplines. Einstein's conclusions are not recognized by many scientific perspectives. Some branches of physics recognize the overall flexibilty of time, yet most of the sciences and all of the histories insist on linear progression. And if fields alone are "real", what are fields composed of? What really is being accomplished here?

In retrospect then, the evolution of quantum mechanics is based on the limiting assumption that energy can be quantified in an objectified manner. Objectivity itself is an artificial methodology that attempts to break down reality into biteable pieces. It is only because of our ego development that "quanta" has appeal. There is no fundamental of energy that will ever be discovered in a laboratory – until the recognition is made that it lies in the understanding of consciousness. And consciousness will not lend itself to dissection and this type of methodology.

Finally, if in Einsteinian terms forward passing time loses its significance – and in terms of quantum theory, particles cannot be pinned down in subatomic realms, does it not follow that the exterior world has the same qualities! Science itself has come to the conclusion that metaphysical writings have been repeating forever, namely that our physical world is an illusion!

Appendix B

QUESTIONS, CURIOSITY & ESOTERICA

The following are a series of questions that arose out of curiosity while pursuing an understanding of Tesla, Einstein and quantum theory.

● ● ●

Question:
(12-15-89) Does Einstein's theory of curved space have any validity?

Not in greater terms. Einstein's conception of space and time in his thinking of relativity was accurate up to a point, being accurate only as it relates to energy and matter, still valid only in the context of your physical perspective. It will be your challenge Michael, to combine these theories of curved space and the ether – arriving at a synthesis with an understanding that both Einstein and Tesla had their moments, but neither understanding the validity of the "illusion" behind both genius's "truths".

Question:
(1-12-90) Anybody out there?

Yes Michael. "I" would like you to create a statement – a synthesis if you will, of the drift of my work as Tesla. Then look at Einstein and do the same. Make reference to how we differed and how we can be merged – considering your understanding of the "illusion" and how it can be merged with the ether & relativity. Here, you will merge physical laws into the input of consciousness . . . relativity into ether and conscious intent, both of which science ignores. Recognize that physical laws are only valid to the illusion of physical perspective, and while curvature of space sounds wonderful to the recollection of a physical model – coming to terms with infinity and a constant creation along with simultaneous time goes much further. Understanding **consciousness as the mother-board,** you can easily work out a system unification – which both men desperately attempted.

Question:

(1-16-90) How do I bridge the gap between Tesla's model of electrical/mechanical vibration at earth's resonance – and our model of "continuous energy"?

Tesla envisioned a system of electrical/ mechanical devices tuned to earth resonance – lending itself for stimulating the electromagnetic fluidity of the earth and amenable to "standing waves" that could be explored further. He believed he had a workable model that indeed could have been explored had he the resources to proceed. Our model, utilizing what Tesla discovered relative to the resonance of the earth, approaches an understanding of "standing waves" as he perceived it.

This whole area can get rather technical, but standing waves here reflects the perfect **balance between waves and particles** – waves "become" particles through conscious intent and interaction with the purposes of exploring a physical perspective. The illusionary aspects of your plane involves the relative intent of whether one is operating from "wave" perspective or a "particle" perspective. Yours is a particle perspective while you are awake and "conscious" in your terms, but a wave perspective is entertained during various altered states of sleep, meditation, and various occasions where you relax and allow your ego to step aside to varying degrees. There is no "real" distinction between waves and particles – for particles are, once again, coagulated thought-forms that offer the opportunity to perceive reality in a physical manner.

The unification of Tesla's research and our model will make more sense to you after you explore a more scientific description of waves and particles – recognizing that in quantum physics the connection is now being made that the distinction between the two isn't as critical as an understanding of the conscious interaction in the experiments themselves.

Question:

(1-16-90) Tesla illuminated his lab with electric vacuum lamps and no apparent "source" of electricity. Was he using some form of our circuits?

"I" was cognizant of electric oscillations created through my coils as creating a force field that could be operable within a short range. I didn't carry this effect out on a grander scale until Colorado (in 1899) – and subsequently had no sufficient financing to pursue this arena.

Question:

(2-27-90) Are Units of Consciousness (U.C.) themselves miniature black holes and white holes?

Yes Michael. Every aspect of physical perspective is ultimately composed of these U.C., and each contains its black hole – white hole counterpart. This is not to say that there aren't seemingly "greater" black holes and white holes "in" space, but again, these are pockets of double space that energizes your system as yours energizes others. The similarity of black holes and white holes to the coordinate points is obvious – and in many respects they are the same. Where coordinate points differ is that they could be considered as a gestalt of U.C. that seeks physical expression, whereas the U.C. themselves have no such orientation as such. They are amenable to a variety of expression, in ways that do not require a physical focus.

U.C. are considered gestalts since consciousness itself is not composed of "units". There is a breakthrough into units with the underlying intent for physical expression. Since each thought you entertain "contains" a coordinate point as its impetus for creation, you can see that you are divine beings indeed, exploring the very process that All That Is utilizes in the creation of "worlds". Your thoughts can be envisioned in this manner, so as to empower your sense of self. When we say that you are divine beings of light and love, you can take that literally. And when we say that your thoughts, as they leave your awareness, create universes for others to ponder – can also be taken literally.

"True science" would entail an investigation into consciousness and the inner universes of the mind. This can not be done with "objective" experiments as such, but with a recognition of consciousness as a variable in these experiments. An unbounded universe defies the imagination and logic in these terms, so must be dispensed with. Here, only consciousness will carry you into a fuller understanding of your world. Curved space seems curved because of the nature of your instruments in exploring light waves through space. Space is curved in this sense, but only in mathematical terms which incorporates the illusion as its basis. Mathematics will only carry you so far, because the consciousness behind the equations themselves are limited by the bounds of logic. Logic as a tool has served you well up until now, but will have to be dispensed with in the exploration of self of which is the only exploration worthwhile.

When a coordinate point is similar to a black hole – white hole, it is already predisposed to physical expression. They can be envisioned in each and every U.C. and in space from your perspective. When viewed "in" space, they offer the illusion of space at the same time that they are the building blocks "of" space. The picture of space as viewed from your physical eyes is a projection of reality that is convincing because of the agreement to interact in this medium. From a greater perspective, space is not apparent and the major coordinate points would appear to be greater concentrations of illusion, packed together in sound and light values that provide the impetus for the the various stages of value fulfillment.

Coordinate points are sources of additional energy in a recycling process. Entropy doesn't apply. When a black hole – white hole is compared to a coordinate point, the white hole is contained "within" the black hole. Electromagnetic properties are propelled into the black hole and accelerated. This continues the process of energy exchange from other systems. A black hole is an inverted white hole in these terms. The re-emergence process itself begins a another cycle of exchange, and the process is continual.

Question:

(3-5-90) Why does Einstein's curved space seem to verify itself in mathematical and physical terms?

The projection quality of your instruments lends itself to curved space because of the nature of light and gravity. In a slowed down version of vibration, "physical light" is not the same as nonphysical light. In your terms, light will bend near a gravitational field because of the nature of your illusion ... slowed down matter is equal to your version of energy, but not equal to an overall perspective of energy in nonphysical terms. The distinction becomes one of the gross acceleration of vibration that entails a physical focus.

Contrary to your typical understanding, light slows down and accelerates simultaneously as it translates into a physical projection. Where this process merges becomes the point where it appears to slow down, but in actuality, has sped up in certain terms and hence will bend back into itself near a physical object (which is also composed of that same "light"). The seeming confusion between different aspects of energy and light will be better understood when your scientists unravel the intricacies of matter and antimatter.

Question:

(5-24-90) Is harnessed fusion(1) a practical approach to solving our energy needs?

No. Fusion itself is an approach that consciously is not easily contained in a "third density" illusionary perspective. The process was utilized in your H-bombs, but the very nature of the destructive capacity of this level of fusion along with the ignorance of the potential of fusion, make it an unworkable solution to your energy needs.

The ignorance involved is one of understanding the mechanics of illusion as it transcends itself, through intent, into a pre-matter consideration of short circuiting certain coordinate point activity –

that further lends itself to an imbalance that strives to balance itself between probabilities. The "between probabilities" is the consideration that offers the potential for yet another probable physical universe that would be a mutant perspective of imbalance. This is a possibility, but not with your current understanding of probabilities and parallel universes. Therefore, we do not envision any useful success in these realms with your current state of affairs or your level of scientific and philosophical discernment.

Question:

(5-31-90) As yet, there has been no satisfactory explanation found for the slowing down of time at high velocities, or the increased mass of moving objects. Any comments?

Time slows down because of an artificially created "vacuum" that alters the seeming passing of time. It is a simulated attempt to alter the fabric of the space-time continuum into another dimension (or vibration) but because it is only a "relative attempt", you have a relative degree of time dilation.

At the speed of light, your time would indeed stand still – and at faster speeds, you would have a time reversal of sorts, but only relative to your understanding of forward passing time. Since time does not really move "forward", it's as illusionary as your assumption of "positive time". Time reversal is more like a status quo of time, where it temporarily "pauses" to consider the intent of the consciousness in question. Worlds of antimatter utilize similar positive time as you would consider time, but the "flow" is altered in some ways that are analogous to time reversal – and to the perspective of the consciousness in question, time still appears to be "positive" or moving forward.

Relative to the concentration of **mass** at relatively higher velocities, here you have a situation that is analogous to a gravitational field artificially being impressed upon tracks of space-time. It is not that the object in question is heavier or more massive from the perspective of "its" consciousness, but to the observer it would appear heavier because of the artificial parameters imposed on its surface due to "friction" and "velocity" that have no real bearing on the mass, but on the instruments in question that are still operating on the assumption of physical perspective (of its space-time continuum).

The atomic structure of the moving object is experiencing a faster vibration on its "outer" surface which makes its vibration speed up, while the inner universe of the object is still operating at a slower vibration – and the net effect is is an over compensation of the inner universe of that object to balance the vibration, with an end result of a seemingly heavier or more concentrated mass at higher velocities.

The nature of the illusion itself is being altered here, similar to a collapsed star that your physicists have speculated upon. The collapsed star and the moving object are only partially collapsed in terms of their relative speed, but again, collapsed or fully operational in physical terms has to be considered in terms of its intent to be reconstructed in the understanding of the exchange of energy and mass (for possible recycling into other universes). Coordinate point activity utilizes relative velocity as well as the expansion and contraction of mass – and, the conversion of mass into energy and vice versa.

Question:

(6-1-90) Is there anything to add to Einstein's assumption of the constant speed of light $E = M$ "C"^{2}?

Yes, Michael. Understand that the constant speed of light is only constant in your relationship to your physical environment. Relativity in these terms has no meaning to a nonphysical focus since concerns of velocity, mass, and time are eliminated. These are considerations of a space-time continuum that can only be described as "mass" and "form" orientated.

It becomes impossible to describe space in cosmic terms unless the understanding of "projection" is dealt with. This is why Einstein's theories beautifully described the nature of physical reality in scientific terms, but could not deal with origins or boundaries, since there are none. Assumptions in one space-time continuum cannot be expected to be valid in another, and assumptions in any space-time continuum cannot be considered valid in a nonphysical world.

In overall terms, your scientists are simply struggling with their insistence of objectivity in spite of their knowing that it can only lead to conclusions satisfactory to "left brain" validity. This leaves no room for answers outside the parameters of logic. The world was not created nor is it maintained by logic.

Logic is a tool of ego development that has less value as your world moves into the fourth dimension. Logic served you well in the early struggle for identity when you couldn't separate yourselves from your environment. Now you are having a hard time separating yourselves from your ego! A balance is being orchestrated in a radical shift in priorities where logic will simply no longer serve you in a constructive fashion without the balance of intuition and emotional knowing.

Appendix C

FINAL THOUGHTS

From an Einsteinian perspective, what this manuscript points out is that the missing variable of particle and field is indeed one of consciousness and an expanding universe – not expanding in terms of space, but in terms of how a dream or an idea expands. As All-That-Is "let go" in a primordial explosion of being, all probabilities became expressed simultaneously. We can place this event in our past, but it continues within the eternal now and the constant creation of all worlds. The laws of the physical universe work quite well in the physical universe, but have no place in explaining the nonphysical creation and its infinite worlds of expression. The physical universe necessitates a conscious, but nonphysical origin. Otherwise, we are caught up in the struggle for beginnings and boundaries.

If we could dissolve the gestalt that forms our bodies, we still exist as consciousness. And each of the units of consciousness engaged in this gestalt, which are themselves gestalts, keep on assembling in varying combinations to create yet further more expansive thought processes which create yet more gestalts. This is a continuing process that seeks all possible manifestations to every thought construction, which is a glimpse of the constant creation and the expanding universe(1). Again, it is expanding in terms of expression, not in terms of space.

In certain terms, science has created mysteries where there are none. "Continuous Energy" has shown the flexibility of the illusionary aspects of our physical focus and how the world can reap the benefits of this knowing. "All That Is" lies within us, with literally nothing outside of ourselves but projection. And to the degree that we recognize that we are playing with layer upon layer of projection, we will free ourselves from the unnecessary search for beginnings, endings and boundaries. We are multidimensional beings of absolute divinity with no separation of who we are and the world that seems to surround us. The sooner we accept our divinity in these terms, the sooner we will unleash the awesome power of our being.

Appendix Notes

Appendix A

(1) "Encyclopaedia Britannica" 1981 edition. Volume 13, page 16

(2) ETHER:

The theory of the ether was very popular among spiritualists until the early 1900's. As originally interpreted, it was thought to be the medium through which light travelled. As a wave, light needed a medium in which to exist. This medium was described as all pervasive, invisible, tasteless, odorless, and in fact offering no physical properties at all. In 1887, experiments were conducted that failed to detect the presence of the ether. It was determined that since the earth moved through the ether, it should be possible to detect an ether breeze. Because this 1887 experiment couldn't pin down an "ether breeze", Einstein used this finding in part to formulate his theories and "officially" eliminate the need for the ether in scientific terms.

(3) "Encyclopaedia Britannica", 1981 edition. Volume 11, page 718

(4) "Tesla: Man Out of Time" by Margaret Chaney. Chapter 6

(5) "Prodigal Genius, The Life of Nikola Tesla" by John J. O'Neill. Chapter 15

(6) THE CYCLE OF THE ATOM:

Niels Bohr's model assumed that the electron of an atom remains in its ground state unless energy is added to it. A more expansive picture of an atom and the electron, is one of a continually vibrating entity that exhibits a state of "time sharing". In the on-cycle of its vibration, the atom is present in our space-time continuum. At its off-cycle, however, it is expressing itself in many other probable universes. The atom is actually not present as often as it is absent because of the many worlds it is simultaneously participating in.

The atom is vibrating so fast and the electron is spinning time so rapidly, that this sharing is not apparent. If the Earth plane's vibration is slower or faster than another universe, it follows that the time sharing itself is unequal in terms of the concentration of energy utilized in each respective reality. This would also allow for the relative perceptions of time and other forms of value fulfillment.

Within this recycling process, the electron is spinning time newly backwards. It is in this manner that simultaneous time begins to make sense. The faster the electron is spinning, the denser the reality in question – and, the slower time is experienced. This follows from Einstein's understanding of relative velocity (not to be confused with faster vibration and a less physically orientated reality).

(7) "The Dancing Wu Li Masters – An Overview of the New Physics" by Gary Zukav. Part 1, Chapter 1

(8) SEEMING CHAOS IN SUBATOMIC REALMS:

The seeming disorder in subatomic realms mirrors the narrow perspective of science in its random attempt to describe these events. Objectivity itself will never open up to the perspective required for an appreciation of the overwhelming order and connectedness of our universe.

(9) EINSTEIN & GRAVITY:

Einstein didn't technically consider gravity to be a force. In his General Theory, he recognized it as a curved field in the space-time continuum, created by the presence of mass.

(10) THE NUCLEAR FORCES:

It is believed that the universe is held together by four major "forces". The strong nuclear force binds the atomic nuclei together. This becomes necessary to keep the protons in place since they would otherwise naturally repel each other. The weak force allows for the transmutation of subatomic particles, and the electromagnetic force holds atoms together in the bonding process with molecules etc. Gravity is sometimes considered the fourth major force, although as indicated above, Einstein thought gravity was a part of curved space and not technically a force. The strong force is more than 100 times greater than the electromagnetic force, and is thought to be the most powerful force in nature.

(11) "Relativity, The Special and The General Theory" by Albert Einstein. Appendix V

(12) PARTICLE SPIN & VIBRATION:

An interesting question never really resolved in quantum theory is why a particle is destroyed by a change in the direction of its spin. There is an intimate connection between spin and the overall vibration of a particle. The spin actually **defines the particle.** Therefore, a change in that spin would simultaneously alter the vibration "and" the parameters of the mass in question. Since the particle is "defined" by its vibration, a change in that vibration necessarily changes the particle! The definition of any physical projection, for that matter, is determined by the vibration of that object. It's not that a particle is destroyed by a change in its spin, as much as it simply finds itself recycled into another time-space continuum.

● ● ●

Appendix B

(1) ATOMIC FISSION & FUSION:

Atomic **fission** is the process of splitting atoms with the resulting release of freed up energy. It represents the breakthrough into the technology of the atomic bomb. Atomic **fusion,** on the other hand, is the joining together of atoms, similar to how the sun energizes itself. In the production of the hydrogen bomb, there is actually a fission blast that provides the necessary heat for fusion to take place. In recent years, the search has been on to harness "cold fusion" in a laboratory for the unlimited energy it could potentially provide.

• • •

Appendix C

(1) COMMENT:

Portions of this discussion on gestalt understanding were taken from a conversation I had with Serge Grandbois as he was channeling "Anderson" – several months before this manuscript began.

INDEX

"There is enough energy for all — if you learn how to approach the issue from the perspective of a source within yourselves. It is that simple, although it will take some re-arranging of your thought concepts to appreciate the simplicity."

Order Form

Postal Orders: Sufra Publications,
P.O. Box 16290
Milwaukee, WI 53216

Make checks payable to: Sufra Publications

Please send ____ copy(s) of Continuous Energy.

Name: _____

Address: _____

City: _____ State: ____ Zip: _____

Cost: U.S. $14.95 / Canada $17.95 each 1-3 books

Discounts: 4-9 books .... 15% off
10 or more ... 25% off

Sales Tax: Please add 5% for books shipped to WI

Shipping: Book rate $1.75 for the first book
and 75 cents each additional book

Payment: _____ copy(s) _____ shipping _____ tax(WI)

Check ☐

Money order ☐

MasterCard ☐ (or) Visa ☐

Card Number: _____

Name on card _____ Exp. Date ____ / _____

For information on a talk or workshop in your area, or future publications in this series, please write to the above address.

Thank you.